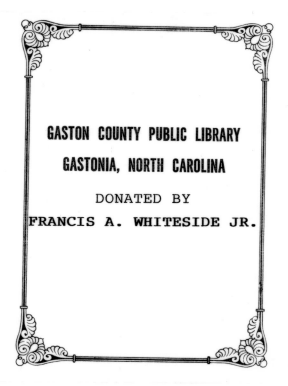

THE ART OF USING
AND LOSING CONTROL

THE ART OF USING AND LOSING CONTROL

Adjusting the Therapeutic Stance

RICHARD G. WHITESIDE

BRUNNER/MAZEL
A member of the Taylor & Francis Group

USA	Publishing Office:	Taylor & Francis 1101 Vermont Avenue, NW, Suite 200 Washington, DC 20005-3521 Tel: (202) 289-2174 Fax: (202) 289-3665
	Distribution Center:	Taylor & Francis 1900 Frost Road, Suite 101 Bristol, PA 19007-1598 Tel: (215) 785-5800 Fax: (215) 785-5515
UK		Taylor & Francis Ltd. 1 Gunpowder Square London EC4A 3DE Tel: 0171 583 0490 Fax: 0171 583 0581

THE ART OF USING AND LOSING CONTROL: Adjusting the Therapeutic Stance

1 2 3 4 5 6 7 8 9 0   E B E B 9 8 7

This book was set in Granjon. The editor was Alison Labbate.

A CIP catalog record for this book is available from the British Library.
♾The paper in this publication meets the requirements of the ANSI Standard Z39.48-1984 (Permanence of Paper)

Library of Congress Cataloging-in-Publication Data

Whiteside, Richard G.
    The art of using and losing control : adjusting the therapeutic
stance / Richard G. Whiteside.
      p.   cm.
    Includes bibliographical references and index.

    1. Psychotheraphist and patient. 2. Control (Psychology)
I. Title.
RC480.8.W49   1998   97-25088
616.89' 14—dc21   CIP

    ISBN 0-87630-863-9 (case)

CONTENTS

PART V: LOOKING BEYOND THE CLIENT

PART VI: MULTIPLE CONTROL PATTERNS

FOREWORD

The Art of Using and Losing Control clarifies complex issues of power and decision making in therapy. Clinicians have always had difficulty describing the various motivations that bring a person to a therapist. Some are driven by despair, others are dragged by their families or ordered to therapy by the court.

Whatever causes the initiation of therapy determines to some extent the individual's willingness to listen to the therapist and to follow suggestions, but it is by no means the whole story. If people were able to follow good advice, most would not need to see a therapist. They would only have to listen to the suggestions of friends and relatives. The problem is that many people cannot listen to good advice and will not follow suggestions.

The art of the therapist is to provide the motivation to overcome this difficulty. This book offers lucid explanations not only of clients' control issues but also of therapists' control styles and how they merge or conflict.

Every therapist will benefit from this book: from the guidelines for identifying a client's and a family's control style in a way that leads to choosing the right strategy for therapy to the special emphasis on illusions of giving control to a therapist to therapists' illusions of being in control of what a client will do.

I was inspired by the examples of using clients' strengths to solve problems and by the strategies for dealing with bizarre behaviors. I intend to incorporate into my teaching the concept of negative diagnosis with difficult adolescents who refuse to collaborate with the therapist in any way. The chapter on oppositional hypnosis is in the best Ericksonian tradition yet it offers original hypnotic techniques.

The best of *The Art of Using and Losing Control* is the conceptualization of the needs of oppositional clients and how to design a therapy that matches those needs, be it hypnotic or indirect. There are many excellent strategies for encouraging clients to hold on to their destructive behaviors and defiance and to use them to overcome their problems. There is an interesting description of situations where a client presents under the aegis of another professional's diagnosis, be it schizophrenia or Attention Deficit Disorder, which marks the behavior as fixed or unchangeable. These are situations in which clients do not relinquish any control to the therapist while at the same time they feel powerless. The book offers strategies for shifting the focus from an intrapsychic to an interpersonal framework and gives valuable ideas to the family therapist about how to accept a colleague's diagnosis to the point of ignoring it. Another factor that makes this book particularly interesting is that it addresses the overwhelming importance of sibling relationships in making and destroying lives.

I believe that every therapist who reads this book will become more curious, imaginative, inventive, and creative.

Cloe Madanes

ACKNOWLEDGMENTS

During the development of this book, a period of five years to a lifetime, there have been numerous forces which have kept me in control by fiddling with the controls while things went out of control. A heartfelt thanks to everyone who has provided inspiration, consternation, and support.

I would particularly like to acknowledge Jay Haley and Cloe Madanes. Many of the ideas presented in the book are a result, either indirectly or directly, from all that I have learned from them. During my years as student and supervisor at the Institute, they were always tolerant of my shortcomings while prodding my development as a therapist. I take full responsibility if I have wandered past where they feel comfortable, since a teacher should never be held accountable for the shenanigans of his or her students.

I would also like to thank all of my colleagues, both former and present, who through their successes and failures have helped me conceptualize my approach. Barbara Peeks was particularly understanding with the beginning of the manuscript, listening to my ideas and questioning them. During my association with Bill Petok, first at Focus on Family, later as a partner in private practice, and finally as a frequent correspondent after my move to New Zealand, I have received encouragement, support, and the latest sports news. I am particularly indebted to Bill and Judith Mazza, for their collaboration on the Malignant Complimentarity and Grandmother Becomes Father cases.

To paraphrase the Talmud, much I have learned from my teachers, even more from my colleagues, but most of all from my clients. Any insights I have obtained have come from my clients' ability to cooperate, rebel, reveal, and share their vulnerabilities. All of the cases included in the book are real. I have always changed names and sometimes changed gender to protect their anonymity. Even where not indicated, all of the cases were followed up after a period of six months to two years to confirm their positive outcomes.

Suzi Tucker, my editor at Brunner/Mazel, provided me with the opportunity to get my ideas to press. Her editorial guidance made a difficult task go smoothly.

And lastly, to my wife, Frances Steinberg, who took time from her own work to assist me with mine. She constantly prodded me out of stubborn ideas and provoked me until I created a better book. Her love, encouragement, and support are more than any one man is entitled. Without her, this book would have remained only an idea.

Richard G. Whiteside

INTRODUCTION

The issue of control permeates all relationships, whether they are personal, societal, or therapeutic. Any interpersonal unit must grapple with the problem of dominance and influence, the assuming or relinquishing of authority. It would be impossible to have human interchange without control exerting an influence on some level.

The word "control," however, frequently evokes images of Svengalian therapists bidding clients to follow their commands. Clients who refuse to comply are labeled "resistant" or noncompliant. Therapists have widely debated ideas about control, authority, hierarchy, and resistance, with views on the subject often colored by theoretical orientation, emotion, and political correctness. Within the realm of social psychology, control has always been perceived as a more positive and necessary construct (Seligman, 1975), with both actions and the perception of ability being related to effective functioning (Langer, 1983). In both perspectives, however, control can be conceptualized as the power held by the person who has the ability to shape the tone, form, or outcome of any interaction.

Therapeutic views toward control have often paralleled society's views. At the incipience of psychotherapy, a time when doctor knew best, father knew best, and teacher knew best, therapeutic models capitalized on the image of a wise, benevolent therapist able to ferret out the client's problem and prescribe a solution. Whether it was under the all-knowing gaze of the psychoanalyst or within the contingency contract established by the behaviorist, the client came to the therapist for guidance, essentially to be told what to do. Rational emotive therapists helped clients change their maladaptive thought patterns; family therapists established interventions to alter the structure or pattern of behavior. No matter what theoretical system was used, the client was perceived as the "patient," the "offspring," the "student" in need of help.

Society changed. In the late 1960s and early 1970s, authority was knocked off its pedestal, women emerged as equal partners, and the rights and needs of all individuals were acknowledged. The therapy world scrambled for a model that was more congruent with this new world view, one that was less authoritarian and more sensitive to patients' needs and rights. Feminist therapy, narrative therapy, and self-help groups all evolved as an attempt to give clients their due, to remove cultural and therapist bias from therapy. Out of vogue were paternalistic, authoritative stances, replaced by more nurturant, encouraging strategies that worked toward the self-empowerment of the client.

Issues of control, however, did not disappear, although often they went underground. Despite a plethora of good intentions, therapists still had to grapple with the fact that simply by sitting in a room with a client, they were likely to have an influence on them (Haley, 1963; Minuchin, 1991). Even if they were to select the most cooperative, empowering, conciliatory stance, a therapist would still be influencing the course of therapy by the choice of technique, the setting in which it took place, and the people who participated. If a therapist chose to sit back and not interfere in family or group dynamics, such passivity would prejudice the discussion in favor of the more assertive participants. Even gentle prodding or questioning could result in a redirection toward topics that the therapist rather than the client deemed important, an assertion of control even if none were intended (Goldner, 1993). In the worst-case scenarios, therapists who abrogated power to their clients would often create invisible (Minuchin, 1991), secret (Haley, 1987), or incongruent (Madanes, 1981) hierarchies, which would lead to poor therapeutic outcomes.

The most seemingly unobtrusive stances, such as the psychoanalyst being positioned behind the couch or the narrative therapist writing a letter to a family, actually have as great an impact on a client as do more overtly directive therapy styles, although often without the therapist's realizing, or at least admitting it. If control involves structuring the tone or form of an interaction, then every feature of the therapeutic interchange, including nonparticipation, has a tremendous influence. Even Dr. Spock came to realize that the best intended unconditional love could still wreak havoc on the child toward whom it was directed.

The ignoring or suppressing of control issues has not led to a resolution of the problem or to better therapeutic effectiveness, a point that is particularly evident when one considers the findings of recent outcome analyses (Beutler & Consoli, 1993; Carr, 1990; Miller, Hubble, & Duncan, 1995; Whiston & Sexton, 1993), which reveal that the most significant factors in creating positive results from therapy lie in the therapist/client relationship, not in therapeutic style. No therapeutic model was any more successful than any other in resolving clients' problems, with all achieving about a 60 percent success rate. It was, instead, the ability of the therapist to match the needs of the client that promoted success.

The time has arrived to drop theoretical and politically correct spins and admit the fact that any time a therapist and client interact there is a pattern of control that profoundly influences the effectiveness of therapy regardless of the approach used. Therapists who insist that they do not encounter any control struggles because they take a conciliatory, supportive role are missing the point. Control is not a matter of confrontation. It is a door to fostering better therapy by accepting the needs of a particular client. Unless a therapist is willing and able to adjust his or her position, therapeutic effectiveness is limited to those clients who match the stances used by the therapist. Most therapy models assume a cooperative client, or at least one who is motivated to change. When a client presents control patterns that do not mesh with the therapist's typical way of responding, the client is seen as nonmotivated, resistant, or unruly, resulting in either unsuccessful or terminated therapy.

A new approach to control is needed, one that is sensitive to the needs of the client and the potential biases of the therapist as they shift across therapy sessions (Kolden, Howard, & Maling, 1994), but that systematically addresses the hierarchical relationship between them. In each phase of therapy, the client's control issues should produce a shift in the therapist's orientation so that the effectiveness of treatment is maximized.

The situation becomes increasingly complex when a family or social unit is involved, since the diverse control patterns within the family force the therapist to continuously appraise the configurations present and develop creative solutions for handling them. Milton Erickson was a master of this shifting of position, Jay Haley expounded on it, but neither ever detailed how to actuate such an approach methodically. Fisch, Weakland, and Segal (1982) and De Shazer (1988) have also discussed the need for therapeutic maneuverability and fit between therapist and client, but have not systematically detailed the client characteristics that should create corresponding therapeutic shifts.

The negative connotations regarding control result primarily from viewing the term as combative rather than as a basis for cooperative effort. Instead, the client's control characteristics should be seen as one of the presenting features of the therapeutic interchange related both to the client's history and to his or her interaction with a particular therapist. Rather than being a basis for confrontation or a means of manipulation, the shifts in control during therapy are analogous to a dance where the tempo of the dance, the length of time spent dancing, and who is leading vary with the type of dance selected and the relative strengths of the partners. Therapy could be a waltz or a tango, depending on the needs of the client and the flexibility of the therapist.

Although therapists are traditionally seen as initially being in a "one-up" position due to their expertise and the fact that clients have not been able to resolve their problems successfully on their own, in fact, both initial and ultimate control are always in the hands of the client. It is the client who asks the therapist "to dance." Clients decide whether to begin therapy, or if they are ordered to participate, decide whether they will attend. Clients also decide how much control they are willing to give the therapist in the resolution of their problems and can choose whether therapy will continue or terminate. Clients have control over how much or what kind of information they will provide to the therapist and how cooperative they will be. However, the level of cooperation is often not a product of client deviousness or pathology, but the overt manifestation of the client's ability or willingness to relinquish control to the therapist.

If control is conceptualized in relation to the outcome of an interchange, then even when a therapist takes a directive, authoritarian approach to a client in order to meet the client's therapeutic goals, the client maintains ultimate power over the situation. The therapist is simply the tool clients are using to achieve their end. The clients allow the therapist to have control over the tone and form of the interaction in order to resolve their issues.

It appears to be a reasonable request for therapists to ask that clients give them relative power and control since the clients are seeking their services and therapists have the education and skills to assist their clients with their problems. The question of who actually maintains control, however, is usually more complex. When clients enter therapy, they are taking a problem that previously had been under their control and entrusting it to a therapist. Clients become vulnerable to the therapist by revealing intimate details about themselves during the sessions. Some clients become embarrassed, resentful, or demanding because they feel inferior to the therapist since they have been unable to solve their own problems and need assistance. In an effort to "save face," many clients refuse to relinquish control to the therapist. Because clients are not bound by an ethical code of conduct, they generally have more flexibility of behavior in that they can cry, get angry, or act sullen during the session while the therapist must use restraint and maintain a professional demeanor.

Since therapists depend on clients to provide information about their current situation and their history, clients often control the therapeutic situation by withholding, fabricating, or distorting information and details that are critical to the therapist's understanding. Clients sometimes suppress information by telling the therapist that no other information exists that is pertinent to the particular problem. A client may do this either deliberately, to manipulate the therapist's understanding of a problem, or inadvertently. Regardless of the client's motivation, therapists rarely work with all of the information at a client's disposal, and so are at a disadvantage in terms of controlling the situation.

Clients may also fabricate details about their situation, often supplying information that is inconsistent with facts known to the therapist. They may do this to show themselves in a positive light, to make themselves look good at someone else's expense, or to avoid the consequences of their actions. Clients may also distort information in an effort to convince the therapist to perceive their problem a certain way. By controlling information, the client can greatly influence not only the direction of the therapy, but also the ability of the therapist to function in a therapeutic capacity.

The tendency to withhold or edit information is not limited to the client in the therapeutic situation. Therapists also modify their verbal output, rarely articulating all of their thoughts about the client, or framing their comments and questions in such a way as to achieve some end. Therapists often do not relay to a client their supervisor's comments about the case, or they may present information in a way that enhances their own prestige.

It is currently fashionable to hold the therapist responsible for whether or not the client is cooperative, attributing any reluctance or resistance on the client's part to the therapist. This perception, however, takes away the client's right or need to be resistant, denying the client ownership of his or her behavior or feelings.

We seem to need a villain. The history of psychotherapy has seen the blame shift from the mother for being too intrusive, to the father for being too distant, to the family for being dysfunctional, and, finally, to the therapist for being insensitive to the needs of the client. This is not to say that therapists don't contribute by their behavior to making clients more or less cooperative. It is only that by taking the responsibility totally away from the client, an artificial dichotomy is created. It appears more sensible that rather than villainizing or canonizing any of the participants, each member of the therapeutic process be assessed as to what role he or she can play in creating a successful outcome.

Ideally, then, therapists must evaluate the level of control a client is willing to give them at any point in the therapeutic process and respond in a way that maximizes therapeutic effectiveness while meeting the client's needs. By adopting such a "transpositional" approach in relation to control issues, therapists are able to adjust their therapeutic stance to achieve beneficial outcomes. Interventions may involve the therapist's taking control, relinquishing control, or using the client's control to obtain results. What is critical for positive outcome is that therapists match their strategies to clients' patterns and issues (Beutler & Consoli, 1993; Miller et al., 1995).

Transpositional therapy should be seen as an overlay, or suprastructure, that can be applied in harmony with many existing therapeutic modalities, rather than as a specified form of treatment. While most systems of therapy prefer a particular stance, the approach detailed in this book should enable therapists, regardless of tradition, to evaluate their own postures with regard to the presenting patterns seen within clients, and to make the necessary adjustments to increase therapeutic effectiveness. In models that already utilize the shifting of stances, the information presented here should provide a means by which their approach can become more consistently successful.

1

PATTERNS OF CONTROL

If a therapist does not have or cannot obtain enough control to influence the client, therapy cannot be effective. By understanding the level of control a client brings to and maintains in therapy, therapists can modify their approach to their client's problems. In the transpositional approach offered here, the client's power is the starting point for the development of a successful therapeutic interaction.

There are primarily four types of control patterns presented by clients in interactions with therapists:

1. Total control   The client defers power to the therapist

2. Partial control   The client defers to the therapist on some issues but retains control over other areas

3. No control   The client refuses to relinquish any power to the therapist

4. Illusion of control   The client appears desperate for the therapist's intervention, but refuses to follow any of the therapist's directions.

In this chapter, these four basic control types are discussed and the therapeutic stance most likely to facilitate a successful outcome for each category is delineated. The initial explanation is in the context of an individual client's entering therapy, so that the basic concepts can be understood. Family and social control patterns will be discussed later in the book.

TOTAL CONTROL

There are clients who enter therapy willing to give complete control to the therapist. This apparent readiness to relinquish control could be a product of their current situation, of their personality, of their cultural background, or of their family of origin. For the therapist, however, total control is a double-edged sword. The cooperation offered by the client enables the therapist to function well professionally but places all of the responsibility for a successful therapeutic outcome directly in his or her hands. A therapist should also be wary of fostering continued dependence in such clients, and by the end of therapy, should conscientiously move the client toward increasing self-reliance.

Among the most typical clients willing to give therapists complete control over the therapeutic process are people in crisis. Clients facing acute, serious situations, such as the loss of a spouse, threatened suicide by a child, or sudden unemployment, are extremely destabilized and anxious for any intervention that will help them feel more secure. Their crisis creates such a high level of discomfort that any solution is perceived as preferable to what they are currently experiencing. They look to the therapist as a stabilizing influence who can provide a way out of their crisis. Because of the inherent fragility of the client at this time, the therapist is accorded enormous influence, which should be used judiciously.

There are also clients whose character is such that they frequently give control of their lives to others, a submissiveness that permeates many of their relationships. In fact, it is often this personality characteristic that brings these clients to therapy, as they frequently have problems with being dominated by significant others, either physically or emotionally. Some clients are willing to give a therapist control because they take a practical attitude toward their problems. If someone suggests something that makes sense to them, they are willing to follow up on it. There is no struggle for control when they are in therapy as they have come to the therapist looking for and prepared to accept practical advice and solutions. Such clients usually are not interested in long-term treatment, and once they are provided with a course of action that they can implement, therapy is no longer needed. In a similar vein, there are also clients who enter therapy with the intention of seeking "expert" advice. They happily place the therapist in an elevated position and expect the therapist to make pronouncements that will better their lives.

The cultural background of clients or their position in their family of origin can also predispose them to give an authority figure complete control. Often they have been taught from childhood that they should respect and listen to anyone in a superior position. The therapist can utilize this framework by adopting a posture that is congruent with the clients' cultural structure in order to resolve their problems. The role that clients assume in their family of origin also influences how cooperative they will be in therapy. Typically, clients who were treated as, and acted as, the "good child," who respected authority, and who always listened to their parents, usually behave in a similar manner with a therapist.

PARTIAL CONTROL

Many clients fall into the category of giving the therapist some control over their problems while keeping partial control for themselves. Once again, the type of control offered can be a product of personality, position in family of origin, or situational factors. The balance of control also ebbs and flows during the therapeutic process (Kolden et al., 1994). As therapy progresses, there are times when the therapist has more control, and the client, by definition, has less. In some cases, clients are initially able to yield sufficient control to the therapist to help them with their situation. If, in the course of treatment, the therapist begins to direct clients to behave in ways that are atypical for them, they may become anxious and need to take some of the control back from the therapist. As therapy progresses and change becomes more comfortable, the client once again can invest control in the therapist and allow the transition to take place.

Clients who have experienced significant trauma earlier in their lives are frequently unable to give a therapist complete control in therapy. Because of the death of a loved one, divorce, or childhood abuse, an individual may have a hesitancy or inability to develop intimate personal relationships. The therapist should be aware that because of their history, these clients can initially yield only partial control of their healing. If the therapist works to build a trusting, caring relationship, eventually these clients can give the therapist more latitude in influencing their lives.

Some clients enter therapy with preconceived ideas about how therapy should be conducted and so restrict the therapist's behavior according to their own expectations. After they explain the particulars of their problem, they then instruct the therapist to resolve it in a specified manner. The technique may be based on something they read or saw on television, or a friend may have mentioned how a problem improved as a result of a specific therapeutic strategy. At times a client may approach a particular therapist and request that he or she repeat with the client an intervention that the therapist had used with one of the client's family members.

These clients only give the therapist control if the therapist agrees to carry out the prescribed course of action. Rather than dismissing the client's potential solution outright, the therapist should listen carefully to the request and use it to gain an insight into what the client really wants from therapy. The therapist can then either accede to the client's direction, if appropriate and ethical, or explain to the client why this situation is unique and propose an alternative, equally successful method.

Ambivalent clients often enter therapy because they are unable to make choices; they feel depressed or confused about what direction to take. Therapy is perceived as a means to overcome these unpleasant feelings and to help them feel happier. In other cases, clients may not normally be ambivalent but their current situation may be so troublesome that they are unable to choose a course of action. All alternatives appear wrong, and they are faced with the decision of remaining in an uncomfortable situation or making a choice they would rather not make. They enter therapy wanting help from the therapist to evaluate their situation and explore possible choices. Ambivalent clients in these positions often give the therapist control in the beginning of the relationship but withhold it when they are faced with having to take action.

NO CONTROL

Some clients refuse to give the therapist any control over the therapy situation. This may be due to their being coerced into treatment, or it may be caused by personality or cultural factors. In these cases, the therapist begins treatment at a considerable disadvantage—cooperation is minimal and opposition is high.

Many clients come to therapy not out of a desire to change some aspect of their lives, but because others are directing them to attend. Perhaps there is pressure to seek help from a spouse, a parent, a school, or an employer. Because the client is attending therapy only to satisfy someone else's demands, he or she is highly resistant.

In more extreme cases, the client may actually be ordered to attend by the court or a social service agency. Such clients primarily attend therapy to escape punishment. They frequently have a history of repeated failures in treatment. They resent being forced to attend therapy and usually acknowledge this fact to the therapist. As a result, they refuse to do anything the therapist suggests and they look forward to the termination of therapy. They exercise complete control over the therapy by refusing to cooperate. Ironically, these clients also feel that they have no control over their own lives or over the situation, as they are being watched and directed by the referring agency.

Some clients seize total control in therapy due to their negative, offensive attitudes toward others. These are individuals who like to assume a superior position and to dominate interactions. They usually enter therapy as if under duress and complain about their problem as though it were separate from them. These clients often state that therapy is a waste of time and express doubt as to whether it will be successful. Their stance is extremely challenging, a "let's see what you can do about this" attitude, with no promise of cooperation. Such clients may have assumed a rebellious, defiant role toward authority figures in their family of origins. This history of defiance may carry over to their adult years and result in their not cooperating with a therapist.

Just as there are certain cultural groups that encourage listening to an authority figure, there are others that feel it is a sign of weakness either to reveal problems or to follow another's suggestions. Some groups, whether fundamentalist christians or teenage gangs, also have specific attitudes as to what information should be contained within a family and what may be revealed to the community. A therapist must be both knowledgable about and respectful of cultural traditions related to the therapeutic situation and use the client's own belief system as a catalyst to effect change.

ILLUSION OF CONTROL

There are some clients who appear desperate for the therapist to resolve their problems and seem willing to give the therapist whatever cooperation is necessary. The therapist sees these clients as willing to comply with whatever is deemed appropriate. Such clients, however, only give the therapist enough control to engage him or her. Once the therapist becomes invested in their problems, these clients withdraw their cooperation and passively resist the therapist's efforts. The client's desperation and need are a mirage that disappears once the therapist approaches. Like magicians, these clients excel in focusing attention on all the wrong places.

Clients in this category often present as desperate, hopeless, and helpless. They have usually been beaten down by their own problems or by those of a family member, and they see no possible resolution. They are often afraid to take steps that lead to change, even if it would make life better. Instead, they develop a "martyr complex" that is carried over into many aspects of their lives.

Clients who offer the illusion of control initially get attention and concern from others because of the intensity and hopelessness of their problem. They often become tiresome, however, and people pull away from them, feeling burdened by the interaction. In response, the client often establishes a similar relationship with someone else until that person also tires of him or her. Many illusion of control clients have several people through whom they cycle to listen to their problems. In reality, the difficulty that others have in interacting with these clients lies not in the severity of the problems, but in the fact that they are usually unwilling to act on any suggestions or to accept any support that is offered.

Therapists generally respond positively to these clients initially and make strong attempts to help them resolve their problems. Since these clients appear to be desperate, like the total control clients in crisis, it appears as though the therapist can take charge of the therapy. As therapy progresses, however, the therapist realizes that although such clients are extremely grateful for the therapist's concern, they will not act on any suggestions the therapist makes. In addition, they begin to extend their control of the relationship passively by being unable to carry out basic tasks in therapy, such as showing up for appointments or paying their bills. When confronted, the clients tell the therapist that they are too overwrought by their problems to cooperate in therapy despite their desperate need for help.

It is possible that these clients may be the product of learned helplessness. Events in their past may have made them despair of having any meaningful control over their lives. They are anxious for the therapist to help them, but wary of relinquishing the last vestige of control they possess, the ability to resist the therapist's direction. Many of these clients have also become so invested in their problems that they are afraid to conceptualize life without them. Frequently, the social and family structure around such people also perpetuates their behavior.

While some ambivalent clients offer the therapist partial control, others who are generally ambivalent in their emotional interactions create an illusion of control. They enter therapy depressed and generally confused about what direction to take. They ask help from the therapist in evaluating their situation and exploring alternative choices. As the session unfolds, however, they become elusive when given any suggestions that will encourage them to make decisions or commitments. Therapist and client usually reach an impasse, as the client feels that nothing is improving and the therapist sees the client as noncompliant.

Illusion of control cases can offer therapists the greatest challenge in therapy. Using traditional methods, these clients elicit long-term interactions where both the therapist and client achieve a high level of frustration, a position particularly noxious under managed care constraints. The client's despair dangles like a carrot before the therapist's nose, prompting him or her to design yet another intervention that will not be accepted.

THERAPEUTIC GOALS

When clients enter therapy, they are usually concerned with resolving a particular issue. Their focus and motivation often center on the specific problem. At times, these issues are revealed directly, such as when a family comes to therapy complaining that their eight-year-old son won't attend school. In other cases, the presenting problem is couched in abstract terms, such as wanting to "feel good" or to have "better communication".

Underlying problems are the network of factors related to the presenting issue in a precipitating or causal fashion. These problems may be concealed from the therapist because they involve sensitive issues. A therapist often ascertains the nature of the underlying problem by examining the context and consequence of the presenting problem or by observing reactions to suggested interventions regarding the presenting issues.

As the therapist ascertains the client's presenting and underlying problems, he or she can begin to establish explicit and implicit goals in therapy. Explicit goals are those problems that are directly affected by the outcome of therapy. Implicit goals are met as an indirect consequence of the therapy. Both explicit and implicit goals are related to the level of control the therapist possesses.

Total Control

In situations where the client gives the therapist total control, the client is generally receptive to what the therapist suggests. The client identifies the presenting problem and the therapist designs an appropriate intervention. In these situations, the presenting problem can be the explicit goal since the client hands the details to the therapist for resolution. If there are underlying problems related to the presenting problem, the therapist can identify these to the client, who can then decide whether they are to be addressed in therapy. If so, the implicit goal of resolving the underlying issues can be approached using the same direct methods as used for the explicit goal.

For instance, parents may initially enter therapy to address a behavior problem in their son. As the presenting problem is resolved, the therapist may speak to the couple about marital difficulties that might be contributing to the situation. The therapist can inquire as to whether the couple wishes additional therapy for the marital problems. As the underlying problems are made explicit, the clients can decide whether or not they want the therapist to help resolve these issues as well.

Partial Control

When a client gives a therapist only partial control, therapy takes on a different tone. It often becomes evident that a client is withholding some control after a therapist has suggested several solutions that are received enthusiastically but are not executed. The therapist begins to realize that the more problems are addressed, the less cooperation is received.

In these cases, the therapist often needs to shift to the underlying problems because they are inherently more potent and thus more provocative. By addressing the underlying problems as the explicit goal and keeping the resolution of the presenting problem as an implicit goal, a therapist can motivate a client toward action. It must be understood that clients generally do not yield more control in the resolution of their underlying problems than they did for their presenting problem. If anything, control might be even more tightly held since the therapist is addressing issues that are more sensitive. It is simply that the presenting problem is not potent enough to effect a change under these control conditions. By addressing the underlying problem in an indirect, non-confrontive manner, the therapist can usually stimulate the client to promote some movement. The situation is analogous to that of a car that is not running smoothly. If the oil is changed frequently, one might get an adequate level of performance. But if you can convince the owner to work on the engine, the results will be more substantial.

A good example of a situation of partial control, where the presenting problem is made the implicit goal and the underlying problem the explicit goal, is the case of the eight-year-old boy who refused to attend school. After several suggestions to help the parents get their child to go to school had not been carried out, I decided to focus on the fact that the father was unemployed but refused to look for work as a possible underlying problem. The topic had been mentioned repeatedly by the parents and was a metaphorical representation of the boy's issues. Two indirect interventions were designed that would use the father's behavior as a motivator for his son's going to school. The father was told he could choose from those two alternatives. In the first, the father would get up at a certain time each morning, dress for work, and spend at least eight hours away from home. This would enable him to model how his son should spend his day and would remove the father as a companion for the son when he missed school. The other approach involved telling the father that he *had* to stay home every day and take care of his son. In addition, he would receive an allowance from his hard-working wife for his baby-sitting. The purpose of this intervention was to redefine the father's staying at home as compulsory with the hope that he would rebel against this role and go to work. This alternative would also make explicit the fact that the wife was working and contributing to the family finances and was unhappy that the husband was not. By shifting to the underlying problem as the explicit goal of therapy, the family increased their level of cooperation because of increased motivation to reach resolution.

No Control

When a client allows a therapist no control over therapy, direct intervention for the presenting problem usually produces resistance and poor results. Instead, the therapist would be more successful using one of the following approaches.

The first approach involves focusing on a problem that is totally separate from either the presenting problem or the underlying problem and making it the explicit goal. The resolution of the presenting problem becomes relegated to the implicit goal of the therapy. For instance, if a couple is assigned to therapy because they have abused their child, the therapist obviously needs to stop the violence. If, however, the couple denies the therapist any control by refusing to discuss their abusive behavior, but will discuss the man's sexual infidelities, the therapist can begin by focusing on the promiscuity as the explicit goal of therapy in an effort to create trust within the therapeutic relationship. After the infidelity issue has been resolved, the therapist will have gained sufficient power to approach the implicit goal regarding the abuse.

Another approach to take with clients who refuse to relinquish any control is for the therapist to take an even more extreme position relative to the presenting problem than the clients take, blending with, rather than opposing, their stance. In this method, clients are positioned to use their tight hold on control to resolve the presenting problem for themselves. The explicit goal focuses on the presenting problem, but in a way that allows the clients' opposition and power to work for them. In these situations, it is best not to address the clients' underlying problems until the presenting problems have been resolved.

> Kenneth, an 18-year-old male, was allowed to attend therapy at the judge's discretion rather than go to court for raping a 13-year-old girl at a party. At the first therapy session, Kenneth refused to admit that he had raped the girl, insisting that the sex was consensual. I read aloud to Kenneth six pages of the police report, including a statement from Kenneth himself saying that he had raped the girl. Kenneth told the me that he hadn't really meant to say that, and he had no idea why he needed to see me for therapy. Several missed appointments later, Kenneth finally showed up, offering various weak excuses as to why he had not appeared previously. I told Kenneth that I had been using the time to consider his case and now agreed that he shouldn't have to attend sessions for something he didn't do. In fact, coming to therapy was like an admission of guilt. I asked Kenneth if he would like a statement from me to give to the judge stating that Kenneth preferred to go on trial for rape rather than attend therapy. Kenneth looked shocked. I reiterated that it was important for Kenneth to stick to his principles so that he could prove his innocence in court. Kenneth began to waver in his stance and confirmed that the police report was true and that perhaps he did need to see me. Kenneth and his family continued with therapy until a mutual termination point was reached.

Illusion of Control

Perhaps the clients for whom it is most difficult to establish goals are those who present an illusion of control to the therapist. In such cases, the clients desperately beg the therapist to solve their presenting problems, even though they will not give the therapist the power to do so. Presenting problems are often described in such general and vague terms as to appear almost meaningless, with the clients expressing a need for "help" or to feel "better," without allowing any concrete goals to be established.

In illusion of control cases, the therapist's explicit goal should be the client's control issues, because the presenting and underlying problems are usually insignificant in relation to how the client interacts in social relationships. The client's presenting problem remains as an implicit goal, but any attempt by the therapist to deal with it directly would meet with poor results. With proper intervention in these situations, clients can take active control over the therapy and their own presenting problems. If additional underlying problems are exposed once a client stops struggling over control issues, they can be addressed conjointly by the client and the therapist.

> Mr. and Mrs. Joy came to therapy because they felt that their seven-year-old daughter, Samantha, was evil and impossible to love. They said that she had been this way since they had adopted her at two weeks of age. When I asked what, specifically, Samantha did that was evil, the Joys described behaviors characteristic of a normal seven-year-old girl. They also regaled me with stories about their son, conceived several months after Samantha's adoption, whom they described as a model child who could do no wrong. Mr. and Mrs. Joy were distraught over Samantha's evilness and begged me for suggestions to help. They swore they were ready to do whatever was necessary to fix the situation.
>
> I suggested several interventions initially, which focused on emphasizing Samantha's good points and resolving the disparity between the parents' views of the two children. The Joys never carried out any of the tasks but came back crying and pleading for my help. At the beginning of the next session, when Mrs. Joy began to moan about how she was cursed, I agreed with her. I indicated that I didn't know how Mrs. Joy managed such a burden, that she indeed had a terrible cross to bear. I also stated that I had no personal knowledge of how to resolve a curse. Since I couldn't come up with any answers for them, I suggested

that perhaps they should act on some of their own ideas, such as hiring someone to take care of Samantha or fostering her out to a relative.

Mrs. Joy called me a few days later, saying that she had found some old home movies. She realized after watching them how much Samantha had changed and that her current behavior was much improved. Mrs. Joy told me that my services were no longer needed since the situation was really not so bad. A follow-up contact from Samantha's teacher a few months later revealed that Mrs. Joy had continued to be more positive about Samantha's work and behavior.

THERAPEUTIC HARDWARE—HOOKS, LEVERS, AND TOOLS

Once one has determined the amount of control present in the therapist–client relationship and established the implicit and explicit goals for the therapy, it is essential to decide on the exact methods that will be used for intervention. The form of the therapy will be in the context of the hooks, levers, and tools the therapist selects.

Hooks are the techniques used by a therapist to get a client invested in therapy and committed to change. Hooks can be positive or negative, embraced by a client or scorned. Therapeutic levers, like their counterparts in physics, are used to gain advantage and move a client from a homeostatic to a change state. By positioning themselves properly and applying leverage, therapists can help clients move toward resolving their problems and changing their behavior. Hooks grasp clients in such a way that they are motivated to change, and levers give therapists a means by which to act effectively. If a therapist has no hook or lever, there is no mechanism for creating change.

A therapist's task, then, is to determine what is important enough to motivate clients to change their current patterns of behavior. The discovery of the proper hooks and levers is usually the result of careful questioning, as well as creative problem solving by the therapist. The changes resulting from using effective hooks and levers are different from those obtained when clients gain "insight" into their own problems or experience a "breakthrough" in their thinking about themselves. Often, clients may perceive their problem in a new way, but still exhibit old behaviors. When hooks and levers are used successfully, a new pattern of action is created, so that clients can respond to their problems in a different way.

Tools are the means by which therapists help clients overcome their problems; they are the interventions or strategies a therapist designs. Working with the client, a tool is fashioned—a plan of action is constructed—in line with the hook and lever previously selected. If control is defined as the power to reach a desired outcome, then even indirect or covert tools, such as paradox or strategic manipulations, enable the client to maintain control over the therapeutic interchange. The therapist's interventions are not devious, but simply the means of helping clients achieve the results that they have requested.

Hooks

Every client has a "hook" that invests them in solving their problems. Their hook is that part of them that makes them most accessible and motivated to change. At times, the hook is readily identifiable and can be gleaned from a client's words or actions. At other times, it is necessary for a therapist to search for a hook. Some clients obscure the location of their hook or disguise it in such a way that a therapist has difficulty finding it. When a hook is not apparent, a therapist must create one that will cause the client to invest in a different way of thinking about his or her problem. This could be done by suggesting a new idea to a client or elaborating on a point that the client had minimized.

Generally, then, there are three primary ways in which therapists would select a hook for therapy:

1. They could use one that a client has presented.

2. They could uncover a hook a client has disguised.

3. They could invent a hook.

The following case is a scenario that further explains the three types of hooks and how each one would be used to motivate a father to spend time with his son.

Scenario 1: Using a Hook That is Presented

A mother comes to therapy and explains to the therapist that her 14-year-old son is depressed because his father appears to be unconcerned about him and seems to prefer spending time at work rather than with the son. The father listens to her statement and agrees with what she is saying. He says he realizes that spending more time with his family would solve his son's problem, and probably strengthen the marriage as well. In this situation, the family is very clear about what the problem is and provides the therapist with the hook of getting the father to spend more time with his son.

Scenario 2: Uncovering a Disguised Hook

A family comes to therapy complaining that their son is depressed. Neither parent admits to having any understanding of why this was happening, and the teenager himself doesn't know why he is depressed. In making inquiries about the family, the therapist notices that everyone with whom he spoke commented on the father's work schedule and how little time he spent at home or with his son. In this case, the therapist uncovers a hook by observing the relationship between the son's depression and his father's spending quality time with him.

Scenario 3: Creating a Hook

A family comes to therapy complaining of their son's depression. Any attempts to link their son's behavior to anything else meets resistance. The therapist commiserates with them, and then asks the father to discuss his relationship with his own father. The father relates how his own father never had any time to spend with him because of the demands of his work. The therapist connects the feelings the father experienced as a boy to his son's feelings about him. In this case, the therapist needs to create a hook for the family. Once the hook is presented, the therapist can watch how the family members position themselves in relation to this issue in order to decide how to proceed with therapy.

The use of hooks in therapy is closely related to the level of control given to the therapist by the client. Clients who give their therapist complete or partial control over therapy are generally more revealing about the nature of their hooks. Situations in which the client gives the therapist no control or only an illusion of control, usually require the therapist to uncover a hook or create one for the client. There is rarely just one possible hook for each client, although at times that might seem to be the case. In each situation, the best hook must be selected, the one that helps the client invest in therapy, so that leverage can be applied.

Levers

Hooks alone are seldom enough to create a change in a client. After a therapist finds out what motivates a client to change, the posture or stance the therapist needs to take in relation to the client should be considered. Levers are used so that a therapeutic fit can be made in the relationship (Beutler & Consoli, 1993; De Shazer, 1988). Whereas hooks focus clients by getting their attention and commitment, levers enable the therapist to take a position to help clients change.

Leverage allows a client and therapist to meet their goals and achieve results in therapy. The amount and type of leverage that a therapist uses should depend on the therapist's and the client's resources, the hook selected, and the amount of control the therapist is given (Allgood, Bushoff, Smith, & Salts, 1992; Beutler et al., 1991; Haley, 1987).

When a client is cooperative, less leverage is needed, as the therapist has control of the therapy. If the client retains more control in the relationship, the therapist must apply the right leverage so that the client can undergo a change with regard to the problem. Effective therapists apply force in proportion to the amount of control they possess; the more authority held, the less leverage is needed.

If a client yields control to a therapist, essentially requesting the therapist to use his or her skill in resolving the client's difficulties, then the therapist can assume a more authoritarian stance. The therapist is able to ask the client to carry out specific tasks to alleviate the problem or to offer specific suggestions. In scenario 1, for example, once it was established that the father needed to spend more time with his son, the therapist could direct that to happen. There would be little opposition from the family since they all had agreed that this was the right course of action. The therapist would be able to give ideas to the father about how to spend social time with his son, how to help his son with any problems that might contribute to his depression, or how to talk to his son about his interests.

A therapist can be authoritative if the client is willing to cooperate or is requesting the therapist's direction. A therapist should also assume an authoritative stance if a client is taking a course of action that is destructive or counterproductive to his or her well-being. For instance, if a couple comes in for marital therapy and the husband informs the therapist that he intends to have an affair, the therapist should tell him directly that this would be detrimental to his marriage.

If a client gives a therapist less control, the therapist must use more indirect techniques, since authoritarian stances would create resistance. Control can be seen as analogous to water in a glass. If the client retains control, the glass is full. It would be foolish for a therapist to "pour" suggestions in; they have no place to go. Indirect techniques serve the purpose of gaining control of the therapeutic relationship without creating a spill. If the correct levers are used, there is no struggle for control, and the client's problems begin to change, resulting in a better client–therapist relationship and a successful outcome.

Therapists often need to assume a yielding posture in situations in which clients have partial control or total control. Since it is subtle, yielding is perhaps the most powerful, nonthreatening method of establishing a relationship with a client. As Lao Tsu indicated in the *Tao Te Ching* (1971), one must often yield in order to overcome. If a therapist yields to the client's power, the client stops struggling for control since no one is fighting them. As a result, the nature of the problem and the quality of the client–therapist relationship undergo a change (Windle & Samko, 1992).

An adolescent boy came to therapy and refused to speak. After several attempts at interaction, I yielded to the client's control by agreeing with him that silence was perhaps the most useful way we could both spend the time. I congratulated the client on realizing that the session could best be spent quietly contemplating all the nuances of the problem. We remained quiet for the entire hour. Toward the end of the hour, the boy started glancing at his watch, but I stayed firm in my decision not to speak, even though I was sure my next clients were in the waiting room. Fifteen minutes past the expected end of the session, the boy stood up to leave. I nodded to him, and he departed.

When the boy arrived for his next appointment, I asked him if we should resume the silence. The young man stood quietly for a moment and then produced some photographs he had taken. He pointed out some areas in the pictures where he felt some aliens were hiding. He told me that he had not mentioned them before, because he was afraid he would be hospitalized if he brought them up. By effectively yielding during the first session, I had been able to develop a relationship and begin the therapeutic process, without grappling for control.

By redirecting client behavior and perceptions, a therapist can also achieve leverage in situations where control is partial or is being withheld. The ability to change the meaning of a behavior or to refocus attention to something not met with resistance is akin to the magician's art of shifting the audience's attention to something unimportant so that a trick can be accomplished. A therapist who is able to redirect a client's attention can maintain the client's integrity and control while achieving resolution of the problem (Erickson, 1964).

Bill came to therapy in a rage. His wife had told him he needed to come because he was driving her crazy with his jealousy. Bill would go ballistic every time he thought about his wife and her ex-boyfriend, Fred. He would scream at his wife, accusing her of sleeping with Fred behind his back, and would actually go berserk any time he heard anyone mention the name "Fred," even if it weren't in relation to his wife's ex-boyfriend. Bill told me that he really didn't want therapy or to give up his jealousy, but he wanted to keep his wife.

I decided to take a redirective stance with Bill and suggested that he buy a roll of stamps and a box of envelopes, and get 100 $1 bills. Each time that Bill had a thought about Fred and his wife, he was to mail $1 to the ex-boyfriend without any note of explanation. If Bill became angry or abusive about Fred to his wife, he was to mail $5. Bill agreed to the plan. The following week he reported that it only took sending $1 to Fred to resolve the issue. By redirecting Bill's jealousy to anger at having to send the ex-boyfriend money, I was able to obtain resolution of his problem without taking control from him.

The stance that a therapist takes in order to create leverage—authoritative, yielding, or redirective—should be determined by the amount of control the client is offering. As the client's control issues shift during therapy, so should the type of leverage used. This is particularly apparent in partial control cases, where the degree of control yielded by the client continually changes during therapy. After determining a hook to invest a client in a problem and deciding the use of leverage, the therapist must choose a particular format for the therapeutic intervention.

Tools

Tools are essentially the form of action that the therapist takes to resolve a problem. The selection of an intervention is essential to effective therapy, since a problem cannot be resolved without solutions that are appropriate for a client's personality and presenting problem. Tools usually get the credit when therapy is successful since they provide the "glamour." There are as many tools available to therapists as their imaginations will allow. Tasks or directives can be outrageous, simple, complex, or blunt. In order for therapy to be effective, however, the tools used must lead to a positive outcome and be related to the established implicit and explicit goals. While interesting to create, tools are dependent on the successful development of hooks and levers. Without engaging a client or positioning oneself to use control effectively, the creative development of tools becomes irrelevant.

In general, three types of tools are commonly used by therapists—core, direct, and indirect. Core tools are the basic skills the therapist brings to every situation. Respect and tolerance are important components of therapist behavior, regardless of client characteristics. Effective listening, the clarification of statements, or summarization are interpersonal strategies generally beneficial to any interchange.

Direct tools are those whereby the therapist asks a client to carry out specific tasks. Such a tool might be directing the client to spend more time with another person, to develop a ritual, to write a letter, or to go through an ordeal. These techniques are best used with clients who have given the therapist control and are cooperative. Indirect tools, such as paradox, reframing, pretending, or metaphor, are generally more successful with clients who present other control patterns, since they allow the clients to hold onto their power without provoking resistance.

Table 1.1 summarizes the relationship between patterns of control and therapeutic approaches. In the next chapter, the ways of identifying control patterns during therapy sessions will be detailed. The remaining chapters of the book provide clinical examples of how this transpositional template can be successfully utilized.

TABLE 1.1
Relationship of Client Control Patterns to Therapy Techniques

	Total	Partial	No	Illusion
Explicit goal	Presenting problem	Underlying problem	Alternate problem or exaggeration of presenting problem	Client's control issues
Implicit goal	Underlying problem	Presenting problem	Presenting problem	Presenting problem
Hook	Obvious hook	Hidden hook	Create hook	Create hook
Lever	Authoritarian stance	Authoritarian or yielding stance	Redirection or yielding stance	Yielding stance
Tool	Direct	Direct and indirect	Direct and indirect	Indirect

2

IDENTIFYING PATTERNS OF CONTROL

CLIENT PATTERNS OF CONTROL

In the transpositional approach to therapy, it is imperative that a therapist discover the pattern of control a client is presenting so that the therapist can adopt a compatible stance. The accurate identification of control style enables the therapist to select appropriate hooks, levers, and tools. This chapter details those aspects of client behavior during the initial contact, the first appointment, and the course of therapy that are indicative of the four control categories. Therapist control patterns are also discussed.

A therapist acquires a great deal of information even before a client is seen for an appointment, starting with a referral letter or a phone call from the client. Referral sources may reveal patterns of cooperation in their own involvement with the client, detail cultural history, or indicate issues of concern. When a therapist contacts a client to make an appointment, additional information can be obtained by observing the client's behavior in relation to scheduling a time for a session, the client's willingness to bring in relevant family members, and the client's general reaction to the therapist. If the therapist's usual procedure is to have the client engage in some presession activity, such as recording the frequency of symptoms, gathering reports, or reading a brochure, the client's degree of compliance with these requests can also provide some indication of control style.

During the initial interview, patterns of control are often revealed in the freedom with which clients divulge information, the openness of their body language, and the phrasing of their problems. Over the course of therapy, the therapist can also learn something about the client's control style from his or her willingness to attempt interventions, follow suggestions, or provide feedback. In the following sections, the patterns of behavior typically seen for each of the control types are described.

Total Control

The client who offers the therapist total control is generally cooperative and compliant from the time of the pretherapy inquiry. He or she agrees to bring in relevant family members and may even make suggestions about other participants who might be helpful, such as a biological father who does not live in the home. The client makes an effort to find a mutually agreeable time for the appointment and in general indicates a readiness to begin therapy. The therapist is encouraged by the client to contact any referral source prior to the meeting. A preliminary relationship is established, and both the client and the therapist look forward to the first session.

> Ms Barker called for an appointment, anxious to find a
> solution for her nine-year-old son, James, who had been
> soiling his pants. Her pediatrician had diagnosed him with
> encopresis and suggested that she call. Ms Barker had
> already given the pediatrician permission to discuss the
> case with me, had signed a release of information, and had
> asked him to forward a report. She said that the doctor had
> told her that I had been successful in treating other
> children in his practice, so she was hopeful that I could
> help James. Ms Barker agreed to an appointment time and
> inquired about what or who she should bring to the
> session. She informed me that James' father lived in
> another town, but gave me permission to contact him as
> she realized that he was an important part of her son's life.

Clients who offer total control to a therapist are usually forthcoming about their problems during the first session. They answer the therapist's questions, ask for clarification when needed, and elaborate on their answers. The session has an air of collaboration, a mutual sharing between client and therapist. The client often defers to the therapist, seeing the therapist as a professional who can help resolve the situation. The client's body language implies that he or she is open and cooperative.

Such clients willingly listens to the therapist and accept any tasks or suggestions with the intention of carrying them out. If they have a point of disagreement or a question about the interventions, they usually indicate this politely so that an explanation or adjustment can be made. They do not present any problems with regard to paying fees, and they are happy to make an appointment for a follow-up session, if necessary. They make arrangements to include any other interested participants in the next meeting.

> Ms Barker and James attended their first session. There was an easy flow of information; they answered my questions without hesitation. They talked openly about their wish to help James stop defecating in his pants. There was a milieu of mutual respect, and a trusting relationship was established. I gave the family some suggestions to work on during the week, and they agreed to try them. Ms Barker gave me permission to invite James' father to the next session, as I thought it might be helpful. Another appointment was made, and they paid their fees and left.

The course of therapy for clients who give a therapist total control is generally briefer than with other control types. Because these clients defer to the therapist, there can be a quick resolution of their problems, provided the therapist is skillful enough to find an appropriate intervention. If the therapist does not have the ability to direct these clients appropriately, therapy will bog down and be ineffective. Total control places the primary responsibility for success in the hands of the therapist.

Follow-up sessions in these total control situations often focus on the client's providing feedback to the therapist about the intervention and the therapist's making the necessary adjustments for the client until a desired outcome is achieved. Once the presenting problem has been resolved, either the therapist or the client can suggest working on underlying issues. The therapeutic contract can be renegotiated, and the underlying problems addressed, in the same cooperative fashion as at the beginning of therapy, with the advantage of having established a positive relationship and a mutual history of success with the presenting problem.

> James, his mother, and his father attended the second and third sessions together. James and his mother described for Mr. Barker the goals they had set for therapy and the strategies they had tried. They told me that they had experienced a good week, and after following my suggestions, James' encopresis had almost disappeared. Mr. Barker was also given a task, to be carried out between the second and third sessions. James and his mother were encouraged to continue their course of action since it had been successful the previous week. The third session found James' encopresis nonexistent and the family more relaxed. During the appointment, the parents talked about their roles in James' life and asked what they could do to be more effective. I suggested some ways in which the family could function more harmoniously. At several follow-up sessions, the family reported continued improvement. James' encopresis did not return, and the therapy was terminated by mutual agreement after the fifth session.

No Control

When a client offers a therapist no control, even the initial telephone call can be trying. The client questions or opposes any comment by the therapist. Appointment times are all inconvenient, and the client does not want to bring in anyone else for the session. In cases in which a child has been referred, the parents in this category insist that the problem is not connected to them in any way. They see no reason why they should attend or participate in sessions; they only want their child "fixed."

If no control clients are referred by an agency or by the court, their conversation is usually peppered with derogatory comments about the referral, clearly impressing the therapist with the fact that they are not attending therapy of their own volition. It is important to note that not all court-ordered or agency-referred clients fall into this category. Many of them consider therapy a welcome opportunity to mend a difficult situation, a contrast to those in the no control category who envision the referral as an unnecessary intrusion. No control clients who are not referred by the court or an agency can also see attendance in therapy as being driven by external forces, whether by a family member or because of some problem that exists independently of themselves.

> Robert, age 10, his older brother, Mickey, age 14, and their parents, Mr. and Mrs. Samuels, were ordered by the Juvenile Court to come to therapy because Robert's probation officer had reported a new incident of stealing. Mr. Samuels made it clear to me on the telephone that he did not want to attend, and wouldn't even consider doing so if he hadn't been forced to. He was adamant that the problem could be fixed by the family and church and was furious that the matter had been brought before an outsider. Mr. Samuels finally agreed to an appointment time, after complaining how the first three slots suggested would interfere with his work or his church activities. He demanded to know how long the therapy would last, repeating that he was only coming because he had to and that he didn't want to attend any more sessions than were necessary to comply with the court order.

When a client refuses to give the therapist any control, the first session is likely to be difficult. Body language is usually hostile or closed, and communication is stilted. There is often an air of secrecy, with direct answers to questions seldom forthcoming. The interchange is punctuated with potent silences or negative comments, and the therapy struggles to keep moving. All suggestions or requests are either countered or ignored. The therapist is constantly asked when the session, and therapy in general, will be over. It is a struggle to keep all of the participants involved. The client complains about any fees, even if they were discussed previously. This is particularly true if an agency has made the referral, as the clients feel that the people forcing them to attend should be responsible for payment.

> Mr. and Mrs. Samuels sat with their arms folded across their chests, alternately glaring at me and staring out of the window. Robert initially refused to come into the room, and after finally entering, he sat in a far corner. When I asked him about his stealing, Robert swore at me, saying that this whole thing was a waste of his time, and that he would rather be with his friends. Mr. and Mrs. Samuels yielded information grudgingly, their comments spaced between long pauses and much hostility. When asked why they were so unhappy to be in the session they reiterated Mr. Samuels' views as expressed in the initial phone call, that the family and church should be allowed to handle the problem, rather than some outsider. Mrs. Samuels added that their older son, Mickey, had also been referred for therapy years ago and that the counseling hadn't stopped him from stealing. The family balked at having to attend further sessions and did not see why they should have to pay for the service. They refused to consider any of my suggestions for helping Robert with his stealing problem, complaining that nothing would be of any use. An appointment was reluctantly arranged for the following week.

Clients who allow a therapist no control frequently do not carry out any tasks suggested during the first session. When they return for subsequent appointments, the feedback they provide is usually terse, consisting of complaints about the problem or having to attend therapy. Any improvement is attributed to some factor other than treatment, since crediting the therapist would mean that the client should engage with him or her. Therapists should keep in mind the approach detailed in Chapter 1 and not give such clients any further suggestions for resolving the presenting problem unless they are sure they will be carried out. Rather, the therapist should concentrate on addressing an alternate issue that the client is willing to discuss or on exaggerating the presenting problem in a way that will engage the client. Trying to be direct or authoritative with clients who allow no control is impossible until you establish a common interest or enhance motivation.

> Mr. and Mrs. Samuels returned to therapy, still complaining about their son's behavior and their desire to address it at home. They stated that discussing the situation outside of their church community was objectionable to them and that any stealing was the family's business and nobody else's. I responded by agreeing with them, talking about how Mickey and Robert have embarrassed the family by behaving in a way that forced the family into therapy, exposing the family's vulnerabilities to people not associated with the church. I suggested that if we were able to get the boys' stealing under control, the Samuels would be able to keep their problems within the home and church once again. The Samuels continued in therapy with the motivation that by doing so they would become free of statutory interference in the future.

Partial Control

Clients in the partial control category alternate between exhibiting signs of total control and of no control, depending on their vulnerability or the phase of therapy. The therapist can observe this shift in behavior at any point in the process and needs to adjust his or her stance accordingly. During the pretreatment phone call, the therapist can assess the initial degree of compliance. The client may challenge the therapist's request to bring in family members, questioning the relevance of or necessity for such action, or may refuse to have the therapist contact the referral source. Other partial control clients appear very complicitous at the beginning of therapy and do not with-hold cooperation until the therapist approaches sensitive issues later in the course of treatment. Partial control clients weave a pattern between the boundaries of total control and no control. It is up to the therapist to pick up the threads being offered to keep the session from becoming unraveled.

Karen called to make an appointment to see me. She said that she was a recovering alcoholic, but that problems with her boyfriend, Gary, were tempting her to drink again. When I suggested that she bring her partner with her to the session, Karen refused, stating that she wanted to handle this without him. I offered Karen an appointment time that week, but she deferred, saying that she wasn't ready to start so soon. We scheduled a session for the following week.

At the first appointment, Karen talked easily about being a recovering alcoholic, but was not forthcoming whenever her relationship with Gary was discussed. Toward the end of the session, she disclosed that Gary was violent with her during sex, and that while his behavior scared her, part of her enjoyed the drama and danger of being with him. I suggested that, for the time being, she needed to ensure her safety by staying away from Gary, at least sexually, and that she should really consider including him in the next therapy session. Karen again refused the idea of his attending and added that she didn't think she wanted to keep away from him. I shifted the topic, asking her about her family of origin and her childhood. Karen was reluctant to discuss any of this, but eventually revealed that she had enjoyed engaging in other sorts of dangerous behavior when she was an adolescent. She hadn't realized before that being with Gary gave her the same thrill. Karen stated that she loved the feeling of danger, but that she didn't want to die. We discussed some other ways she could achieve excitement that would not endanger her life or cause her to relapse. Karen agreed to consider them.

Over the course of therapy, we worked on redirecting Karen's thrill seeking into ways that were more acceptable to her. She eventually established a relationship with an eccentric man, whom she later married. Karen stated that his spontaneous behavior gave her a rush similar to that achieved by engaging in dangerous activities.

By allowing clients their initial hold on control and by shifting to the underlying problem to invest them in therapy, therapists can help clients who give them partial control to achieve a successful outcome. With these clients, as with all clients, the therapist must continually appraise the level of control offered so that the most appropriate therapeutic stance can be selected.

Illusion of Control

Initially, clients in this category present as total control clients, exhibiting many signals similar to those clients who come to therapy in a crisis. It doesn't take long for the differences between the two to emerge. During the pretreatment phone call, illusion of control clients seem desperate, expounding on the seriousness of their situation. They carry on a lengthy conversation, making sure the therapist understands the magnitude of their problem. These clients often refuse to even consider bringing other people to the therapy sessions with them, since no one else has been suffering as much as they have or has been able to help them. They usually do indicate, however, that their family is supportive of their going to therapy and anxious that they receive help. Illusion of control clients often speak glowingly of their referral sources, all the while complaining that the person who made the referral had been unable to fix their problem. These clients plead to have the next available appointment, but then defer it, rejecting any suggested time as inconvenient. Bemoaning the delay, the illusion of control client asks the therapist for suggestions as to what to do until the appointment. If the therapist complies with the request and offers advice, the client counters each idea proposed with reasons why it won't work. The therapist ends the conversation with the feeling of already having conducted several sessions with the client, and they have all gone badly.

> Mrs. Yarrow called to schedule an appointment for her 15-year-old grandson, Mark. She and her husband had taken care of him since he was a baby. She told me that Mark had joined a white supremacist group, denouncing his Jewish upbringing, and aligning himself with his father's heritage. Mark had also threatened to blow up the library of the private school he attended and had provoked some of his black classmates to the point that they fought with him. Mrs. Yarrow said she was at the end of her rope, that she was too old to cope with so serious a problem. When I asked whether her husband could do anything with Mark, Mrs. Yarrow said that he was tied up with business matters right now and wouldn't be able to attend the therapy. Mrs. Yarrow begged me for an appointment as soon as possible, since the school had suspended Mark in response to his bomb threat. I offered two times the next day, neither of which was acceptable to Mrs. Yarrow, and she indicated that it might be better if she brought Mark in the next week. She wanted to know if I could think of any suggestions to keep him under control until then, and asked if I would attend a meeting at the school in two days concerning Mark's reinstatement. I explained to Mrs. Yarrow that I would not be able to go to the school until I got to know Mark and his family. She agreed to bring him to my office the next day.

Illusion of control clients come to their first session anxious for help. They often state that they have already tried "everything" and complain about other therapists who were unable to achieve a positive result. When asked about their problem, they respond vaguely, offering no clear insight into their situation or any specific goals they want to reach. Every attempt by the therapist to focus such clients makes them even more elusive. The only fact they are sure of is how miserable they are. Their body postures fluctuate between pleading openly and being dramatically passive.

By the end of the session, the therapist is struggling for a way to provide closure to this ephemeral interchange. The therapist's best efforts are confounded, however, because illusion of control clients are known for "door handle" revelations. With a hand on the knob poised for an exit, the client brings up a significant or startling fact, such as having been raped as a boy by his father. This can prompt even the most insensitive therapist to sit down and go over the details, thereby running late for the next session. It is as if illusion of control clients are sentences with commas, but no periods. If the therapist finally achieves enough control to end the session, the client professes being unable to pay and is unsure as to when he or she can come back.

Mrs. Yarrow and Mark came to the first therapy session, prior to the meeting at the school. She explained that Mark had been having problems periodically for the past year, but that things had become much worse after he said he was going to blow up the library. Mrs. Yarrow caught Mark networking with a white supremacist group on his computer Internet program. Mark laughed at his grandmother's distress, telling me how cool it was to be part of the group, while punctuating his speech with racial slurs. When the therapist asked them both what they hoped to accomplish with therapy, Mrs. Yarrow said she just wanted Mark to be normal; Mark stated that he wanted his grandmother to chill out.

Suggestions about what to do with Mark's interactions with the white supremacist group and his violence were cast aside by Mrs. Yarrow, who said she was too upset to try anything, that she was too old for this, and that she just couldn't cope. As the session ended, Mrs. Yarrow told me that her insurance would cover only a small part of the fee and that she could not afford the co-payment on her budget. She then reminded me to meet her at school the next day. Just before she left, Mrs. Yarrow asked if I thought it was important that the reason Mark had been left with them to raise was because her daughter had run off with a member of the KKK. I told Mrs. Yarrow I would see them at the school tomorrow.

Illusion of control clients engender growing frustration in therapists during the course of treatment as they refuse to try any of the suggestions presented but continue to complain. As the client despairs, the therapist struggles to find an even better intervention, hoping that this time he or she will be clever or competent enough to help the client out of difficulty. Illusion of control clients have trouble keeping their scheduled appointments, but frequently demand the therapist's attention between sessions, often calling to ask for help with an impending crisis.

The therapist also begins to develop feelings of powerlessness and helplessness, eventually rivaling those of the client. As a result, the therapist may turn on the client, blaming the client for the impasse. Before the situation reaches this level, the therapist should refocus the therapy onto the client's control issues rather than continually attempting to resolve the presenting or underlying problem.

I attended the school meeting, at which, to my amazement, it was decided to reinstate Mark. By the time I had returned to the office, Mrs. Yarrow was on the phone, hysterical because, on their way home, Mark had told her he planned to attend a white supremacist rally. When I said that I would discuss it with her at the appointment later this week, Mrs. Yarrow informed me that would be impossible since she would not be attending therapy. Coming to the sessions was too stressful for her, so she would just drop Mark off. If I needed to speak with her about anything, I could call her after the appointment.

I saw Mark for the session and discussed his interest in the white supremacist group. A short time after he left, Mrs. Yarrow called to find out what happened and what she should do about Mark's attending the rally. I told her that I required more information to help Mark properly. I suggested that she continue monitoring his computer activity and that perhaps her husband could attend the rally with Mark. When they had gathered sufficient information about the group and Mark's involvement with it, they should all come in for an appointment. Mrs. Yarrow called two weeks later to tell me that after her husband had attended the rally with Mark, Mark had stopped contacting the group on the computer and was getting along better in school.

To summarize, therapists gain a wealth of information about clients' control styles during all phases of their interaction. Table 2.1 lists the key indicators for each control type across the course of treatment. By correctly identifying the pattern of control that clients present, therapists can position themselves more effectively.

THERAPIST PATTERNS OF CONTROL

Clients are not the only ones who bring a habitual control style to the therapy situation. Many therapists, by virtue of their theoretical orientation, personality, or experience, have typical ways of responding to clients. If a therapist's style is rigid, the client's problems will be resolved only if the pattern of control fits with the therapist's orientation. A therapist utilizing only a single stance will meet with either success or difficulty, depending on how congruent that posture is with the client's characteristics or needs.

Total Control

Just as clients give total control of the therapy over to the therapist, some therapists yield completely to their clients. Total control therapists allow the client to decide virtually all aspects of the therapeutic relationship. They establish few, if any, parameters of the therapy, allowing clients to decide the course of the relationship and how their problems will be approached. Therapists in this category frequently ask such questions as, "How do *you* think you should respond to your spouse?" or "How

TABLE 2.1
Patterns of Control Across Therapy

	Total Control	No Control	Partial Control	Illusion of Control
Pre-appointment characteristics	Information freely given; cooperative attitude regarding appointment times, participation of family members; eager for help; referral source indicates a compliant, motivated client	Information withheld; resistive attitude regarding appointment times, participation of family members; does not want or need help; referral source often mandates appearance	Information selectively withheld; hesitant about making appointment or bringing in relevant family members; wants help but on own terms; referral source sometimes indicates significant history as underlying issue	Information almost overabundantly given; changes mind frequently about appointment time and possible participants; desperate for help, often requesting a preappointment solution to problems; long history of unsuccessful attempts to solve problems with other practitioners
Initial session characteristics	Information given freely; smooth rhythm to therapy; suggestions willingly accepted; mood is collaborative	Short, terse, responses to questions; erratic rhythm to therapy; suggestions refused; mood is combative	Information is given freely on some topics, withheld on others; rhythm can be smooth and then disrupted; suggestions are questioned and evaluated; mood is hesitant	Information is vague with allusion to a "secret"; rhythm fluctuates between engagement and frustration; suggestions are refused but client begs for more help; mood is frustrating
Subsequent session characteristics	Good feedback used to fine-tune previous suggestions	Little feedback or compliance with suggestions from previous sessions	Variable feedback and compliance with requests depending on the issue	No compliance with suggestions or accurate feedback but an increase of desperation

would you like to proceed?" Rarely are concrete statements put to the client, as this would mean the therapist would be taking a position. Total control therapists will sometimes make direct comments, but these are used to emphasize what the client has said or wants.

Therapists whose goal it is to empower others or who do supportive therapy frequently fall into this category. Offering total control to clients is also used by beginning therapists, who are fearful of taking a position with a client, concerned that in their inexperience they will damage the client by making the wrong statement or suggestion.

This control pattern works best with illusion of control clients since these clients seek help in taking control of their lives. By supporting their quest, the therapist avoids any confrontation or frustration and allows a productive interchange to occur. Giving total control to a client works worst with those clients who wish to give total control to the therapist. In this situation, both participants want the other to direct the therapy. When total control clients try to give a reluctant or supportive therapist the authority to help them, and the therapist returns the control to them, the clients become frustrated and discouraged. Therapist and client assume the roles of Alphonse and Gaston, endlessly deferring to each other and never making it through the door.

To a lesser extent, clients who allow the therapist no control or only partial control also have problems with a therapist who wants them to have total control. The no control client comes to therapy with an authoritative attitude, and does not need more power from the therapist, unless it is the power to leave. If the therapist is able to empathize with the client in their desire to get out of therapy, this can have a positive effect. While partial control clients may be initially grateful for the therapist's support, at some point they want the therapist to assume enough authority to help them with their problems.

I recall a supportive therapist who ran an agency that helped families with a wide range of problems. She was well regarded in the community and had a reputation for being loving, hugging her clients through their ordeals. She often had difficulty collecting fees from her clients as that conflicted with the supportive position she took with them. Her clientele grew, as many of the families stayed with her, basking in her affection but not getting any better. The therapist became frustrated and bitter, overwhelmed by her clients' growing needs and her lack of compensation.

No Control

It is hard to believe that some therapists give the client no control in the therapeutic relationship. However, this traditional, authoritarian posture is more common than one might assume. It can be found in therapists who have adopted a superior stance because of years of experience or due to their status in a particular system of therapy. These therapists typically ask the client only enough to get a grasp of the problem before pronouncing what should be done. Follow-up sessions find these therapists questioning the client as to the success of their interventions, often blaming the client if they have not worked. Clients are urged to try harder or better to follow the directions of the therapist if they wish resolution of their problems.

Clients who have a tendency to give a therapist total control do very well in this relationship as they are seeking expert direction. Some partial control clients also succeed with these therapists, as they may respond to the therapist's power and feel secure in the relationship. When partial control clients wish to assert themselves, however, they resent not being given the opportunity to do so. No control and illusion of control clients do the worst with this type of therapist. The interaction with the no control client often becomes combative, as the therapist and client try to dominate each other. Illusion of control clients become increasingly helpless with these domineering therapists, frustrating the therapist with their noncompliance.

I once supervised a therapist who always insisted on allowing his clients no control over therapy. He would devise tasks for them and tell them not to schedule another appointment until the tasks had been completed. The therapist felt he shouldn't have to help a client who was not willing to listen to him or execute his plan. As a consequence, he rarely had to deal with resistant clients; they simply didn't return.

Partial Control

Perhaps the most flexible and adaptive way for therapists to position themselves is to give some control to their clients, and retain some for themselves. Partial control therapists can be either authoritarian or yielding, asking questions or making comments as appropriate. The dialog between the therapist and client flows, each deferring to the other as necessary. As stated earlier, it is important that the therapist match his or her posture to the client's, with both proper timing and fit.

Most experienced therapists are capable of this type of control, having confidence in what they have to offer and respect for the client's needs in the relationship. Partial control therapists can be effective with clients who present any of the four control types, although they can have problems with no control or total control clients, if they do not adjust their stance at the right time. When a client comes to therapy looking for an expert, it is not the moment to be humble or deferential. In doing so, you might lose the authority that you wish to exhibit at a later time.

I remember doing a hypnosis session under the supervision of Jay Haley. Afterwards, he commented that I had spent too much time inquiring about the client's problems before I hypnotized the client to help with a phobia. As I reviewed the tape of the session, I could see that by the time I had finished my interview, the client had become insecure in the situation, a fact that made the induction much more difficult. If I had responded to the client's cues at the beginning of the session instead of following my own agenda, the hypnosis would have been more effective.

Illusion of Control

This type of therapist is the least common of the four control styles. Two kinds of therapists, in general, fall into this category—those who strive to maintain control despite their ineffectiveness and beginning-level therapists who attempt to posture as an expert despite their insecurities. Like their client counterparts, illusion of control therapists appear eager to help, but do so in a manner that entails the least amount of professional risk. These therapists are frightened of losing control and so insist that therapy be done their way. Unfortunately, they never clearly define what that is for the client and refuse to be pinned down for suggestions. Illusion of control therapists show up late for appointments because of their fear, and make it a practice to involve other professionals in the treatment, which gives them a sense of security. They often think their clients are "out to get them" in some way, whether by entangling them in custody decisions or impinging on their time. Of all the control types, those therapists are generally the most vulnerable and the most at risk. While they may spend endless hours at self-improvement seminars or in study groups, they rarely seek the type of supervision or training that would effect real changes in their capability to treat clients as this might expose them as less than expert.

Illusion of control therapists often seduce clients by fueling their expectations that they will help them. They ask penetrating questions, make statements about their own expertise in the client's problem area, and appear to be supportive. As with illusion of control in clients, this behavior is essentially a facade, and the therapist rarely delivers. In fact, when the therapy begins to stagnate or fails to reach resolution, the therapist turns on the client, using sarcasm or denigration to mask feelings of inadequacy.

Although basically ineffectual with all four control types, these therapists work best with clients who give them partial control. At some point during their interactions, the therapist's vulnerability and incompetence match the client's desire to take charge of his or her own problems. Some illusion of control clients like this type of therapist because they dance the same dance. However, clients who wish to yield total control become very frustrated with illusion of control therapists, whom they see as evasive. They object to the therapist never taking a substantive position with regard to their problems, often filing complaints that the therapist refused to act on their behalf. No control clients usually find such therapists intolerable, a confirmation of all the reasons they didn't want to attend therapy in the first place.

Illusion of control therapists have a need to control paired with their vulnerabilities. Because of this, they often strive to get out of direct practice and into an administrative role. In that way, they can posture as experts without having to face clients.

I once worked in a clinic with an illusion of control therapist. He liked to impress the staff with his superior knowledge and academic background, but then would plead for help on any difficult case. He always thought that parents had it in for him if they demanded treatment or asked for help, and he felt traumatized when dealing with children. He insisted on having a co-therapist on complex cases, or dumped his failures on other staff members. His helplessness sometimes engendered coddling by members of the team, but when it was paired with an authoritarian air during sessions, the families in treatment complained. He finally moved into an administrative position in the agency.

Both therapists and clients bring styles of control to the therapy session. Table 2.2 summarizes the relationship between the patterns in terms of therapeutic outcome. As therapists, we bear the responsibility for making the relationship work. This requires a constant monitoring of the control patterns exhibited by the clients we see and a continuous appraisal of our own behavior.

TABLE 2.2
Relationship Between Client and Therapist Control Styles

Client Gives Therapist	Therapist Gives Client			
	Total Control	Partial Control	No Control	Illusion of Control
Total Control	Disaster	Variable	Good	Frustration
Partial Control	Workable but weak	Good	Fair	Fair
No Control	Good	Good at times	Ballistic	Disaster
Illusion of Control	Good	Fair	Disaster	An interesting dance

3

TRANSFER OF POWER

Historically, therapists have used their authority to empower clients, helping them to gain control of their lives and resolve their problems. As described earlier, this ability to use a direct approach is much more effective than yielding or redirection in situations where the client prefers to take a one-down position. Assumption of control by the therapist often leads to an efficient and successful resolution of the client's problems when it is managed properly, but it can also have less beneficial outcomes.

Therapists can manipulate a client's vulnerability and abuse the power they have been given, as when therapists take advantage of a client sexually or financially. In other instances, therapists may relish the feeling of power and use it to victimize clients emotionally, putting them down and not letting them get back up.

The ultimate goal of an authoritarian approach should be empowered clients who are better able to take control of their lives because of the successful resolution of their problems. The therapist does not need to become subservient or ingratiating in order to accomplish this. By stabilizing the client and fostering better patterns of dealing with his or her situation, equalization should be achieved.

Consider the metaphor of two glasses of water. If a client enters therapy in a crisis or with a serious problem and wishes to take advantage of a therapist's skill, that client could be perceived as an empty glass next to the therapist's full one. By the end of the therapy, the client should have water in his or her glass, but it didn't necessarily have to come from the therapist's container. If the therapist maintains his or her status but helps the client, both should be able to have full glasses when treatment ends. In other words, the goal of therapy with clients who give the therapist total control should be successful resolution of the client's problem, thereby producing a more competent, capable client.

METHOD

This chapter presents a number of cases in which the therapist uses an authoritarian approach with total control clients in a way that leads to positive outcomes with regard to the client's problems and the transfer of power. As mentioned previously, this is best achieved by focusing on the presenting problem directly, making it the explicit goal of therapy. Once successful resolution is accomplished, the therapist can shift to addressing the underlying issues, if the client is interested in doing so. In some cases, therapists can tackle the underlying and presenting problems simultaneously. The issues are linked, and thus by working on one, the other is fixed. For example, a therapist might ask a mother to give up drinking to set an example for her teenage son who is abusing drugs.

The methods described in this chapter are designed for clients who are cooperative. In addition to giving the therapist the control to solve their problems, these clients are invested in therapy, so there is no need to uncover hooks or create them. The therapist is able to use direct interventions, requesting the client to perform specific tasks that lead to successful outcomes. By following the therapist's instructions, the client solves their problems and emerges as a more powerful, less stressed individual.

The essential components of the approach are:

1. Clients give total control to the therapist to solve their problems.

2. Clients are specific as to whether they wish resolution or insight.

3. Therapists, after assessing the dynamics of the presenting problem, direct clients to perform a task that is in opposition to the cause of the problem.

4. Clients are capable of performing the task and are invested in therapy.

DESPERATELY SEEKING STEVE

I was fairly surprised when Brenda, a 34-year-old medical colleague, asked me for an urgent appointment, stating that she was shaken and feeling suicidal. We had collaborated in the past on a number of chronic-pain clients, and she always exuded confidence and an infectious sense of joy. Brenda managed a slight smile when I arrived to escort her to my office, but it was clear that she wasn't her usual self.

For the first 20 minutes of the session, Brenda described the past nine months of her life. A false claim by one of her clients, and the subsequent impact on her malpractice premium, had forced her from private practice into managed health care. Two weeks after she changed jobs, her husband ran off with her best friend. After she initiated divorce proceedings, he began to call her, threatening to harm her if she didn't sell their house and give him half of the profits. One month after her husband left, Brenda's grandmother died, and six weeks after that, her mother went into the hospital for kidney surgery. Somehow she had persevered through the worst of it, and had even managed to establish a relationship with a new man, Steve. It was problems with Steve that finally pushed her past the coping point.

Steve presented as solid and stable, a safe haven that could help her recover from her past traumas. At least, he had begun their relationship that way. Lately, he had become radically ambivalent. One day he would tell her how much he wanted to marry her once her divorce was finalized, and, the next he would say that he didn't want to see her so often because he was afraid of becoming involved. Brenda was reeling from the inconsistencies. Every time she would position herself, Steve would do an about-face, and expect her to do the same. Brenda found herself continually adjusting and readjusting her plans and her emotions. Two evenings earlier, Steve had called and told Brenda to pack as he wanted to take her with him on a business trip the following day, saying it would be more fun if she were along. Brenda made the necessary adjustments to her schedule and packed before she went to work. After finishing with one of her patients, she saw a note on her desk. Steve had called and canceled the trip. Brenda rang him at his home, catching him on his way out the door. When she asked him what had happened, he screamed at her, saying that she was like an albatross around his neck. Steve said he was leaving and that he shouldn't have to explain his actions to anyone. When he hung up the phone, Brenda fell apart, the tribulations of the whole past year crashing down on her. She felt suicidal, unsure whether she wanted to go on in a world where she couldn't trust her personal judgment. Brenda had thought she had known her ex-husband, her ex-best friend, and now Steve, only to find out how wrong she was. It made her feel unlovable and stupid.

It was clear from her monolog that Brenda was coming to therapy in a crisis mode, anxious for answers and a restitution of her life. She stated that she had called me because I had given so much help to our mutual clients, and prayed that I could do the same for her. It was evident that Brenda was giving me total control of the therapy. She was openly forthcoming about both her underlying and presenting problems, and while she was obviously invested in the process, it was clear she expected me to do something to help her.

Given this situation of total control, I initiated therapy with the explicit goal of stabilizing Brenda with regard to her current difficulties in her relationship with Steve. I began by focusing on her presenting problem in the context of her underlying issue of not trusting herself. I asked Brenda if it were her normal way of interacting to continually adjust her plans and emotional positions because of somebody else's behavior. She managed a laugh, saying that usually she was so sure of herself that the opposite typically happened, that she expected people to adjust to her. Brenda said that in the past she had always taken the approach that if she believed a course of action were right, she would see it through, although she didn't think she was inflexible in this. If someone gave her a good reason for changing her behavior, she would adjust her position, not because the person had said to do so, but because she now had a new understanding of the situation. Brenda said that she had achieved so much personal and professional success in the past that she had learned to like and trust herself and was generally centered.

Brenda's whole demeanor changed when talking about her usual way of interacting with people. She looked much more like a confident colleague and less like a victim. I asked Brenda what she would do this week if she were acting like her old self. She said that since she had arranged to have time off, she would probably visit an old friend in another state, then she wavered slightly, worrying about not being there if Steve called to apologize. I asked her again if waiting by the phone is something she would have done before this year. Brenda laughed and said she has always been too busy to spend her time sitting around waiting for something.

Brenda returned for therapy after her trip. She said that being in another place, having fun with someone who loved her, had helped her gain perspective. We discussed ways she could react if Steve were to act ambivalently in the future. Brenda said she felt capable of confronting Steve about his behavior. When I spoke with Brenda a short while after terminating with her, she indicated that she was doing well and had ended her relationship with Steve shortly after we terminated therapy because he was not willing to behave in a way that met her needs. Before the end of our sessions, I asked Brenda if she wanted to work on her feelings of insecurity or any other underlying problems she was having. She declined, saying that she now felt strong enough to deal with issues on her own. Brenda wasn't denying her problems, she said, but wanted to handle them herself.

In this example, Brenda entered therapy in a crisis and gave me total control because she trusted my ability and needed stabilization. After following the suggestions made during the direct intervention, Brenda felt empowered and ready to resume control of her problems.

MOTHERLESS CHILDREN

I received a call from Jeff, a father of two children, Amy, age 15, and Mark, age 9. Jeff, said he felt that his children had been having difficulty adjusting since the death of their mother in an automobile accident a year earlier. He said the situation was compounded by the fact that he and their mother had separated three years before the accident, and she had received custody of the children. Until the accident, Jeff saw Amy and Mark only during weekend visitations. He reported that initially after the separation he and his wife had been openly hostile toward each other, but in the year before her death, their relationship had been more civil. Jeff wanted an appointment to help resolve the problems he and the kids were having since they had come to live with him.

During the first session, the family openly discussed the mother's death. Mark was tearful during the conversation, but Amy was outspoken and opinionated, stating that the worst part was not her mother's dying, but having to live with her father. She described Jeff as a male chauvinist pig, a loner who smoked too much. Amy felt that her father never took the children's feelings into account, but just did things his own way. This was particularly evident when Jeff decided that they would move to a bigger house in a distant neighborhood without considering the kids' complaints that they wanted to be close to their friends. Jeff said he took them back to their old neighborhood every weekend to play with their friends, but felt that the new house would be more comfortable for all of them. He was upset because the kids never helped clean the place, and he dreaded coming home to disorder every day.

Amy told me that she had frequently helped her mother because her mother had discussed such matters as finances and family problems with her. She felt her father treated her as a child and so she acted like one. Jeff agreed with Amy, saying that he behaved that way because he thought the children would want their father to take care of them. He hadn't wanted to burden them with problems, so he had deliberately avoided giving them responsibilities. Jeff explained that he hadn't wanted Amy to have to take on the role of wife during her teenage years.

The family was very clear in describing their issues and feelings. They also made it evident that they expected me to provide them with solutions to their problems. I used a direct approach and told them that they all needed to invest more with each other. I told Amy that if she were used to taking responsibility with her mother, then she owed it to her father to help him as well. Amy was asked to list the areas in which she would like input, and she readily mentioned finances, groceries, managing arguments, and helping Mark. All three members of the family helped to draw up a list of responsibilities and discussed what role they would play in relation to each one. The mood of the family shifted from anger and depression to one of expectation and cooperation.

Therapy continued for several more sessions. The family provided feedback about what had worked and asked me for help in making adjustments where needed. Gradually, the control shifted back to the family as their expectations about being able to solve their own problems increased.

SIDING WITH FATHER

Mr. Parks phoned for an appointment, stating that he was in desperate need for therapy since his son Roger, age four, was so out of control that his wife was threatening to leave. All three members of the family came in the next day. Mr. Parks began the session by stating that Roger never behaved for his mother. When asked what Roger did that caused his wife distress, Mr. Parks replied that he never listens when his mother says "no," but argues with her and then does whatever he wants. When Mr. Parks comes home from work, he attempts to mediate the problem, but his wife always complains that he sides with Roger, which leads to them arguing with each other.

Mrs. Parks said that her husband doesn't realize how difficult Roger is because he isn't with him all day. She said she knew that when she worked as a corporate secretary before being laid off the previous year, Roger's behavior hadn't seemed bad to her either. It seemed much worse since she had stopped working. I asked Mrs. Parks where Roger stayed while she was at work, and she told me he had gone to day care. The center said that sometimes Roger behaved aggressively, but he had never been asked to leave. Mrs. Parks had been trying to find another job and was frustrated by her inability to do so. She was upset that her son did not listen to her, but saw her husband's undermining of her actions as the main problem. She and Roger couldn't stand each other right now, but before they had been close.

The family displayed a high level of openness and cooperation in their providing of information, so I felt that an authoritarian stance was appropriate. I told the family that I had an idea how they could solve their problem and asked them if they would be willing to try it. I asked Mrs. Parks how long Roger could argue with her before she lost patience with him. She said that she could usually endure it for about five minutes before she felt like strangling him. I suggested that five minutes be set as the limit for his complaining. Mrs. Parks was to listen unemotionally to Roger for up to the five minutes, but whenever his arguments lasted longer than that, Roger and his father would have to do something nice for her. Mrs. Parks was to make a list of things she would like, and she could choose one of them whenever the five-minute period was exceeded.

Mr. and Mrs. Parks agreed to the plan. Roger wanted to know what would happen if his mother had instigated the fight. I said it didn't matter who was at fault. Roger had five minutes to voice his objections, and then he had to quit. It was agreed that his mother's watch would be the official timekeeper and that she would show him the starting and stopping times.

When the family returned the following week, they reported there had been one incident, and that Roger and his father had cleaned the bathroom to compensate Mrs. Parks. Mr. Parks commented that Roger had mostly supervised while he did all the work. The following week, Roger had again persisted in his argument, and the family had to take Mrs. Parks to her favorite restaurant for dinner. After these two episodes, there were no more incidents of extended arguing. Therapy was terminated after four sessions.

I had taken an authoritarian stance with regard to the presenting problem, the fact that Roger's actions were making his mother feel like leaving, and established an explicit goal of improving his behavior so that the mother would stay. One of the underlying problems, the fact that Mr. Parks sided with Roger, was made an implicit goal. The direct intervention used the existing coalition between father and son, but in a manner that produced a better outcome. By the end of therapy, the family felt able to deal with their problems outside of the therapy setting.

A MAN WITHOUT A COMPANY

A business executive called to make an appointment, stating that he was concerned about losing his company, as well as his sanity. At the initial appointment, Aaron, age 55, told me how he had built up his insurance agency from a single office in a small town to six locations in the region. He had served on regulatory boards for the state and had even attained some national recognition. Aaron had recently merged his company with the largest insurer in the state, becoming part of a network of over

200 offices. All had gone well until he had a disagreement with one of the other partners about the direction the company was to take. Aaron said that he was basically a small-town boy, with small-town values regarding playing fair. One of the other partners had a similar background, but the third, the one with whom he was having problems, was slicker and more ruthless. When they reached a stalemate in their negotiations, the sophisticated partner suggested that they bring in an outside consultant to take over as CEO. Predictably, the new CEO sided with the slick partner and gradually worked to move Aaron and the other partner out of the picture. Aaron was given no responsibilities, no secretary, and eventually not even a parking space.

Aaron was dejected and depressed. He said that whenever the slick partner would undermine him during meetings, Aaron would lose his temper and do something irrational, which would give the man even more control over him. He worried about his future, but he didn't think he could stand staying in the company, even if it meant losing his pension.

I took a direct approach with Aaron, telling him that he could not undo the past or revoke the merger, but that I could give him some ideas as to how to protect himself from the ruthless partner. I gave him three tasks centering on his behavior at work and at meetings. The first suggestion was for Aaron to contact his cousin, whom he had said was much more cunning than he was. He was to sit down with his cousin and develop a list concerning how Aaron should act when at work. The second task was for Aaron to call his connections state and nationwide, informing them that he was interested in reactivating his collaboration with them. This would provide Aaron with constructive projects even if the CEO would not give him any work to do for the company. It would also demonstrate to the CEO and the ruthless owner the level of power Aaron held in the business community. The third task suggested was for Aaron to bring his lawyer to every meeting in the company, as a show of strength and as a means of preventing Aaron from acting impulsively or angrily. Aaron said that the fees would be expensive, but it would be better than signing important papers that were not in his interest because he was annoyed.

Aaron accomplished all three tasks. His cousin told him to dress sharply, never to drop his head or avoid eye contact, and to act as if all the other owners were his inferiors. The state regulatory agency welcomed Aaron's input, so he was able to spend his days more productively. By having his attorney present at meetings, Aaron was able to negotiate a reasonable pension settlement and an acceptable buyout contract.

Aaron's desperation allowed him to seek a therapist's direction, even though he was used to being in control. In this case, as in the previous ones, it was demonstrated how a therapist can use the authority clients give them to resolve clients' issues before transferring power back to them. By the end of treatment, both therapist and client are empowered as a result of the successful resolution of the issues and the productive therapeutic interaction.

4

BIZARRE PROBLEMS, SIMPLE SOLUTIONS

During the course of practice, a therapist encounters clients with a range of relationship, family, and personal issues. While the variations on these themes are infinite, and each presents its own challenges, many of the cases fall into predictable patterns—the loss of a spouse, a difficult child, marriage problems, empowerment issues. The therapist grows comfortable within these domains and develops a catalog of resources and techniques that have been helpful with certain problems.

There are times, however, when clients present with problems that are highly unusual, even bizarre. The therapist is shaken out of a typical pattern of responding and often compensates by attempting interventions as atypical and complex as the client's behavior. While creative indirect techniques may be useful in partial control or no control situations, for a client with strange behavior who proffers total control to the therapist, outlandish solutions often lead to a poor outcome.

Many clients with unusual behavior offer total control because their actions have produced a crisis situation in their family or social context, and they require urgent assistance. The therapist can become distracted by the bizarre nature of the client's problem, however, and miss the fact that the client is being cooperative. In most of these cases, the clients can be effectively helped by the use of direct, simple interventions, techniques that utilize the client's control stance and normalize the situation. In the following examples, it is demonstrated how clients with unusual behaviors, and who offer the therapist total control, can be helped using common sense rather than complex solutions.

HUNGRY CHILD

Tammy, age nine, came to therapy with her biological father, George, and her stepmother of six months, Jan. Tammy's mother, Eve, lived in another state, and Tammy only saw her at Christmas and during summer vacations. The family explained that for the past six months Tammy had been receiving psychiatric treatment, but the medication had not produced any positive results. The only other counseling Tammy had received previously occurred when during her visits to her mother, she accompanied Eve to her therapist. Tammy also attended a camp for emotionally disturbed children when she spent summers with her mother.

George explained that there had been no problems with Tammy at home, but her behavior at school had been strange. Jan, the stepmother, taught at the school Tammy attended, so teachers were always coming to her with their concerns about Tammy. They reported to Jan that Tammy would spontaneously start to make strange sounds, then drop to the floor and begin chewing the legs of her chair. At first, her classmates thought Tammy was funny, but as time went on, they became afraid of her. Tammy also had a habit of hugging her classmates with such force that they would start crying. Academically, she was doing very well.

Tammy presented as a disheveled, but likable, young girl. She talked about how much she loved going camping with her father and was happy that he had married Jan. She became very animated when telling me about being the flower girl at the wedding. Tammy also talked about how much she missed her biological mother and how she looked forward to visiting her. George interjected that although Tammy always wanted to visit her mother, while there, her enthusiasm would wane, and she would eventually return home earlier than planned. He also expressed concern that Eve placed Tammy in a camp for emotionally disturbed girls, and he did not like Tammy seeing Eve's therapist.

George said he never had developed a deep relationship with Eve, and had impregnated her on a weekend pass from the Navy. He had not even heard from Eve until Tammy was four years old and Eve was hospitalized for depression. George obtained custody of his daughter at that time. He stated that he did not generally believe in therapy, but he was concerned about Tammy's behavior at school and wanted help in altering it.

Jan was very talkative during the session and appeared more anxious about Tammy than was George, partly because she worked at Tammy's school and so received the brunt of the complaints from Tammy's teacher and the principal. Jan said she believed that she and Tammy had a good relationship and was stymied by the situation at school because Tammy's behavior at home was never bizarre.

The family readily gave me permission to talk to Tammy's teacher. Mrs. Watkins was forthcoming during our conversation and described the behavior in detail. The principal and the school psychologist had instructed her to ignore Tammy's outbursts, saying that the girl's oddities should be tolerated because she was emotionally disturbed and not capable of controlling herself. The principal felt that a special school would be a more appropriate placement for Tammy, but her father refused to consider it.

I asked Mrs. Watkins what she would do to address Tammy's behavior if she had not been told to ignore it. She stated that she would forbid Tammy from behaving like an animal. If Tammy persisted, she would inform her that such behavior was unacceptable in a classroom because her actions affected the other students and made it impossible for Mrs. Watkins to teach. Classroom discipline measures would be carried out as necessary. I told the teacher that this seemed to be an appropriate response. When I presented her idea to the parents, the principal, and the psychologist, they all agreed to try the approach, and Mrs. Watkins was asked to implement her plan. The chewing behavior and rolling on the floor happened twice the first week. By the second week of the intervention, Tammy had ceased exhibiting all of the bizarre behaviors.

During the therapy sessions, I asked George and Jan to work with Tammy on defining acceptable and nonacceptable hugging. The family, including Tammy, found the exercises enjoyable and continued the practice at home. Tammy particularly liked to direct who was going to do the hugging. George, normally an undemonstrative person, followed Tammy's instructions willingly, and Jan commented that Tammy was enjoying the extra attention.

I received permission to call Tammy's mother, Eve, before Tammy left for vacation. Eve was initially defensive when I suggested that

Tammy attend a fun camp rather than a therapeutic one. I told Eve that while Tammy might have needed such an environment in the past, there had been such improvements as a result of everyone's efforts, including hers, that Tammy was ready to try a more normal environment. Eve would be instrumental in preventing any relapse and could monitor Tammy's well-being. By the end of the conversation, Eve capitulated and was looking forward to seeing her "new and improved" daughter.

George said he felt the next step should be to get Tammy off her medication, since it hadn't produced any positive effects, and the dryness of her mouth was making Tammy uncomfortable. I called the psychiatrist, who refused to consider decreasing her medication. George was furious and said that he would simply stop giving the pills to Tammy. I convinced him to go consult his pediatrician to ensure that there would be no complications from withdrawal. Therapy was terminated a short time later.

In this situation, Tammy's bizarre behavior and complicated psychological history could have generated a complex, extensive intervention. Instead, by using the control the family and school provided, simple straightforward suggestions were implemented that eliminated the problem. A follow-up with the family a year later revealed that Tammy continued to do well.

HAVE LOVE, WILL TRAVEL

I received a frantic phone call from Mrs. Turner to the effect that her 16-year-old son, Adam, was suicidal and behaving very strangely. An emergency appointment was scheduled for a short time later. The family came into the office in a high state of tension and anxiety. Mrs. Turner explained that Adam had begun mutilating his arm with a knife after his girlfriend of four months had broken up with him. She reported that Adam had been very well adjusted before this. He made good grades in school, had nice friends, and acted politely to his parents and others. Mrs. Turner was very concerned with Adam's current behavior and expressed fear that he might seriously injure himself or commit suicide.

Mr. Turner was also upset. He stated that his work as a truck driver kept him away from his family more than he liked, and he was afraid that his frequent absences had fueled Adam's depression. He said he knew that both Adam and his wife resented his not being more accessible.

Adam sat silently throughout his parents' discussions. When I asked him directly what he thought was happening, Adam said that since his girlfriend dumped him, life at school had been unbearable. He was tormented by seeing her there, and his friends teased him unmercifully. Adam said he just couldn't take it anymore, that all he could think about was wanting to harm or kill himself.

Because of the seriousness and urgency of the situation, the family clearly offered whatever control was necessary to address the situation. A direct approach was needed, one that focused on the presenting problem of self-mutilation and suicidal thoughts, while also stabilizing the family within the context of their underlying issues of separation.

I expressed my concerns to the family and stated that Adam would be best served by getting away from his present situation. I empathized with Adam about how painful life at school must be right now, with his having to face his girlfriend and listen to his friend's taunts. I asked the family if they could see any way to arrange a change of scene for Adam.

Mr. Turner said that he was supposed to leave on a delivery trip within the next few days, and that he would love to have Adam accompany him so that they could talk and reestablish their relationship. Adam brightened considerably at the thought of the trip and saw the whole idea as a bit of an adventure. Mrs. Turner expressed the belief that Adam would be safer in the truck with his father than at home and agreed to contact the school to get permission for Adam to take several weeks off.

Two weeks later, the family returned to therapy. Mr. Turner recounted how Adam had been so emotionally exhausted for the first few days of the trip that he slept for the most of the time. After that, they passed the time talking, and then sharing jokes and stories. Adam said that he had really enjoyed the time with his father. When he got back to school, his friends were just interested in hearing about his experience and didn't mention his being dumped. Even his ex-girlfriend told him how much she had missed him and suggested getting back together.

Adam replied that he didn't think it would be a good idea, that his time away had given him the chance to think about their relationship, and that he agreed that it was right to go their own ways.

Adam and his family continued to improve during the course of therapy. After dealing with their crisis, they wanted to work on the underlying issues involving Mr. Turner's work. While Adam had gained some insight into what his father's life was like when he was away, he still resented his not being home. Mrs. Turner was also able to voice her loneliness and isolation to her husband. Mr. Turner listened to Adam's complaints and his wife's despair. As a family, they decided he would change to local employment, even though it meant a reduction in income and a change in lifestyle.

By being given control by the family, I was able to assist them in stabilizing their crisis situation and eliminating Adam's disturbing behavior. This was accomplished by the development of a straightforward plan that enabled both Adam and his father to gain some status— Adam with his friends, his father in the eyes of his family—while removing the context that was perpetuating the problem. Once the crisis was resolved, the family was empowered to tackle their underlying problems.

BACKED INTO A CORNER

John, a 15-year-old boy, came to therapy with his mother, Nancy, and his stepfather, Paul. The family had recently bought a house in a different neighborhood, forcing John to leave the school and friends he loved. John said he missed his old school and was finding it difficult to adjust to a new environment in the middle of the academic year. His grades had plummeted, so Paul, his stepfather of five years, had restricted John to the house for extended periods. Paul was a huge, intimidating person, so John readily obeyed him, but he hated being grounded because it interfered with his participation in a rock band for which he played the drums.

Nancy concurred with John's analysis of the situation and stated that she never wanted to intervene between John and his stepfather as she felt that parents should present a united front. She added that the family had come for therapy primarily because, over the past six months, John underwent episodes of baring his teeth and making sounds like a wild animal. This frightened her and everyone else in the family. Nancy stated that she and John had always had a good relationship and mentioned that John also got along well with his biological father, whom he visited every second weekend.

Paul explained why he felt his use of discipline was necessary. He said he believed that John needed to see his school work as having priority over his band practice. Since John was barely passing his courses, he needed to use his time to concentrate on his homework. John conceded the point, but stated that his stepfather's monthlong groundings were excessive and restrictive. Paul described how he had allowed his two sons from a previous marriage to run loose when they were failing in school, and they never turned around. He said he wasn't about to make the same mistake with John and was determined to do better as a father this time.

Only John and Nancy attended therapy for the second session. While Nancy had sat silently for much of the first appointment, she now talked freely about being torn between John and Paul. Nancy explained how she felt a need to side with Paul although her loyalties lay with John. Suddenly, John began to growl, baring his teeth like an angry dog. Flinging his chair backward until he fell against the wall, he braced himself there and snapped at me and his mother. I asked John what I could do to help him. He snarled that he wanted us both to leave the room. Nancy and I stood outside of the door for the 10 minutes it took John to calm down.

When we restarted the session, I spoke in a calm voice while indicating that several changes must be made in the current situation. First, John needed to change schools. If it were impossible for him to return to his original school, the family should find an alternative suitable to all of them. Second, grounding could no longer be used as a discipline measure. If John's poor school work needed to be remediated, it must be done in a positive manner, such as by hiring a tutor. Third, Nancy had to relate to Paul what had happened during the session and ask for his compliance so that John's behavior would not return. Finally, Nancy, not Paul, would be responsible for John's school performance. The next appointment was scheduled for a time when Paul could also be present.

When the family came to their next session, Paul explained that he never dreamt that his punishments were responsible for John's strange behavior. He agreed to my plan and actually seemed relieved that he didn't have to correct John's performance at school. Paul stated that he and John had experienced a good relationship until the school problems emerged, and he was looking forward to once again becoming John's friend.

Several subsequent sessions were held. The relationship between John and Paul continued to improve, and Nancy expressed relief that she had her family back. John re-enrolled in his old school and began achieving at an acceptable level. During the last session, he brought a recording of his band for everyone to hear. A six-month follow-up revealed a continuation of the positive outcomes and no recurrence of John's symptoms.

By using the family's cooperation, a plan could be implemented that addressed John's bizarre behavior. John's actions were similar to those of a cornered animal, so strategies had to be employed that ameliorated his feelings of restriction. The family responded well to the direct, clear instructions, because they normalized the situation and provided a way out of the pattern. Even though Paul initially was not as compliant as Nancy and John, he readily agreed to the plan as the seriousness of the problem escalated. While Paul's authority was decreased, it was replaced by an increase in stature due to his improved relationship with both John and Nancy.

In the cases described, atypical behaviors were addressed with ideas for straightforward, simple solutions. Because the families proffered control to the therapist, direct interventions were possible that stabilized and normalized the situations. In situations where clients exhibit patterns of no control or partial control, indirect strategies might have been more beneficial. In cases where clients give total control to the therapist, less is often more.

5

NEGATIVE DIAGNOSIS

Traditionally, when clients appear in therapy acting defiant or oppositional, therapists undertake a series of conciliatory actions in the hope that they can ingratiate themselves with the client and thus achieve cooperation. Obsequiousness, however, rarely impresses a no control client, and the therapist is usually held in more contempt for any efforts at appeasement. Instead of responding to these clients as if they will eventually cooperate, therapists should accept the clients' control postures and position themselves accordingly. As mentioned in Chapter 1, clients who offer no control to the therapist are most successfully helped if the therapist magnifies the client's presenting problem or addresses issues that are more acceptable to the client.

One common group of no control clients are rebellious teenagers. This population frequently treats therapy with disdain and sees the process as irrelevant and intrusive. Adolescents in this category rarely seek help for themselves and only attend therapy at someone else's direction, whether the court, a school, or a parent. Teenagers make it clear to therapists that they are not interested in their assistance and would not be in therapy if they had any choice in the matter. They resist any overtures by the therapist as they see this as a compromise of their position.

In this chapter, three clients are presented—a delinquent, a substance abuser, and an anorexic—to demonstrate how the exaggeration of a presenting problem into a "negative diagnosis" can lead to successful outcomes with uncooperative adolescents.

METHOD

Some therapists use the diagnoses specified in the *Diagnostic and Statistical Manual of Mental Disorders*, fourth edition, (DSM-IV), to classify a problem or fit a client into a category. Once the diagnosis is made, the therapist either discusses the condition with the client, educating the person about the syndrome, or designs a treatment plan in line with the guidelines for the disorder. In the negative diagnosis method proposed here, a sham disorder is constructed that encapsulates and exaggerates the presenting problem of the client. This newly created diagnosis becomes the focus of therapy as the adolescent uses their defiance to rebel against the label.

This particular method is appropriate for clients who offer the therapist no control, those who refused to engage with the therapist when conventional approaches were tried. It is used with the intent of helping a client overcome problems and should not be utilized to disempower the client. This technique also should not be employed out of anger or frustration, as it requires a dispassionate, analytical demeanor to be successful. In this approach, the therapist must adopt an accepting, observational role regarding the client's problem, and this cannot be accomplished if the therapist has reacted emotionally to the client's noncompliance. The technique of negative diagnosis is a creative solution to the client's problems, not a penalty because the client refused to cooperate with the therapist.

Initial attempts at engagement with the client should be attempted. If these are unsuccessful, then several criteria should be established before the technique of negative diagnosis is implemented:

1. The client must be demonstrating sufficient emotion, usually anger or rebellion, to mobilize a reaction to the diagnosis.

2. A family member must be available to take a supportive role.

3. A diagnosis must be constructed that is an exaggeration of the presenting problem.

4. The diagnosis must encompass the theme of the behavior in order to categorize it.

5. The behaviors related to the diagnosis must be observable on a daily or frequent basis.

6. The diagnosis must employ words that help to hook the client into therapy.

MALIGNANT COMPLEMENTARITY

Bill and James were referred by their probation officer to a drug and alcohol treatment program for repeat abusers. Bill, 16 years old, had been expelled from school a month earlier for smoking marijuana on school property. He had a two-year history of marijuana use, but had never been involved with the police prior to the school incident. Bill performed well academically when he exerted the effort, but that rarely happened, according to his teachers and parents. He loved to read classic American and British literature on his own, however, and had an avid interest in how things worked in his father's garage. Bill was extremely rude in his interactions with any authority figures, calling his parents and teachers names and ridiculing their behavior.

James was a year younger than his brother and showed many of the same traits as his sibling. Like Bill, he had a history of marijuana use and acted contemptuously toward adults. Although James had not been suspended from school, his performance there was unexemplary and unmotivated. James typically smoked at parties and with his friends.

Mr. and Mrs. Briggs, James' and Bill's parents, appeared to be overwhelmed by their sons' behavior. Mr. Briggs worked as an engineer and had an easygoing demeanor that rendered him helpless in dealing with his children. When his sons would hurl barbs at him during the sessions, he would not take any action, except to look desperately at me for help. The Briggs had been married for 18 years. Mrs. Briggs worked as a customer relations clerk at a local department store. She seemed amused at her sons' behavior, and particularly enjoyed it when the boys attacked her husband.

Family therapy proceeded slowly. Because of Mrs. Briggs' reaction to her sons' behavior toward their father, I began by trying to get the parents to work together to affect Bill and James' attitudes and drug use. This resulted in little change and no lasting effects. Despite persistent efforts at engaging the boys, it was clear that Bill and James did not want to be in therapy and alternated between treating the sessions as a joke and reacting with hostility. The probation officer had ordered mandatory urinalysis, and the brothers would purposely urinate on the outside of the bottle or toss the sample to me without capping it properly. All in all, therapy appeared interminable, ineffective, and messy.

After consulting with my colleagues at the center, I decided to try the negative-diagnosis approach. Knowing that the brothers frequently alternated their symptoms on a weekly basis, with Bill having a dirty urine one week and James the next, we agreed to tell the family that the boys suffered from malignant complementarity. The syndrome was described to the family, highlighting the alternating symptomatology. I explained that Bill and James had such rude, disrespectful attitudes because they had to wait two weeks before they could display their symptoms. The family was also told that a similar diagnosis had been made in Italy by one of the members of the Milan group, and the discovery had made the therapist famous. I let them know how excited I was that the disorder had now been seen in the United States and assured the family that all of us were likely to achieve notoriety as well.

Mr. and Mrs. Briggs were asked to chart the stages of the disorder, looking for clues as to when it might next occur. They were to write down their findings and bring the results to the therapy session each week. I assured them that nothing had worked previously because the disorder had not been properly diagnosed, and that normal solutions were inappropriate for so rare a syndrome. Mr. and Mrs. Briggs agreed to document the pattern of behavior.

Bill and James were furious at everyone's excitement and angry that I was about to become famous at their expense. They refuted my diagnosis, so I carefully detailed all of the symptoms of the disorder—the hostility toward authority figures, the poor school performance, the use of addictive substances. Mr. and Mrs. Briggs were asked to note changes in any of these behaviors throughout the week.

When the family returned to therapy, there was an astonishing change in the brothers' behavior. Both Bill and James had drastically modified their attitude, and there were no more positive urines. After several weeks of improvement, the focus of the therapy shifted to the underlying problem, Mr. and Mrs. Briggs' relationship. Mrs. Briggs complained to the therapist that her husband ignored her and was insensitive to the fact that her state of health required him to help out more. Mr. Briggs agreed that he had not participated equitably in their relationship and asked for help in how to pay better attention to his wife. Therapy was terminated after a month of marital counseling.

In this case, the technique of negative diagnosis allowed the therapist to accept and modify the brothers' noncompliant behavior. Instead of acting directly, a yielding posture was taken, allowing the therapist to assume an accepting, almost anthropological, attitude toward the behavior. By becoming part of the investigative process, the parents increased their status, with their roles as recorders, an improvement over their previous position of ineffective, frustrated authority figures. A follow-up with the probation officer two years later revealed that the case had been closed because no further problems had been identified, with Bill and James maintaining continued improvement in their attitudes and school performance.

SYMBIOTIC INTERCONNECTION SYNDROME

Trevor, age 15, attended therapy with his mother, Pearl, at the request of his high school guidance counselor. The referral was the result of Trevor's continued disruptive activities in school and his mother's inability to control him at home. Trevor had been caught shoplifting in a grocery store and was sentenced to community service by the Juvenile Court. The counselor mentioned in the referral that Trevor's parents had divorced five years earlier. Trevor's father, who had a history of alcoholism and spousal abuse, was now living in another state, so the boy had little contact with him.

Trevor showed up for his session in an angry and agitated state, indicating that he had no use for the entire process. A tall, gangly boy, he was hostile to everyone who spoke to him. Every attempt I used to gain rapport was rebuffed, and every question was met by either no response or an angry retort.

Pearl remarked that she was forever having to force Trevor to do things, whether it was getting out of bed in the morning or doing his homework. She said that her job as a pharmacist was in jeopardy because she frequently had to leave work to attend school conferences whenever Trevor got in trouble. While Trevor had friends, he was often at odds with them and spent much of his time around the house, being sad and angry and screaming at his mother. Pearl said that no matter what she tried, Trevor responded with hostility. Trevor complained that he never had any freedom, that his mother was always directing him about school, his friends, or his appearance. Her constant nagging, he said, drove him crazy.

Pearl had tried to carve out a life of her own since the divorce. She said that her social life was adequate, if not thriving. Her relationship with her mother had also improved recently. Pearl had been a headstrong teenager herself, and when she had run away to marry Trevor's father at the age of 19, her mother had disapproved strongly.

I strove to establish rapport with Trevor, seeing him individually and discussing his interests in music, commiserating with him about having a nagging mother, and empathizing about his missing his father. Trevor responded to each attempt with contempt, saying that I didn't know what I was talking about. When I asked Trevor if he could enlighten me as to what was actually happening, he swore at me and said that it was a waste of time and money to be here.

I helped Pearl develop realistic expectations for Trevor's behavior and gave her suggestions as to how to enforce limits. Several sessions later, Pearl reported that all of her efforts had been useless, since whenever she tried to enforce a consequence, Trevor told her to go to hell.

I decided that Trevor's continued noncompliance was appropriate for a negative diagnosis intervention. I told him that it had finally become apparent that Trevor was suffering from symbiotic interconnection syndrome (SIS). I explained how most teenagers who were 15 years old preferred to be independent from their parents, and didn't want them involved in their life. Adolescents usually run in the opposite direction if a parent wants to spend too much time with them. Instead, Trevor's SIS kept him dependent on his mother.

Trevor looked horrified. He became quite emotional and demanded that I tell him how I came to this conclusion. I made a list of the symptoms that led me to my decision:

1. His mother wakes him up every morning instead of his using an alarm clock.

2. His mother fixes him breakfast instead of his getting it himself.

3. His mother goes to school to get him out of trouble because he can't solve the problems himself.

4. His teachers communicate with his mother about his work because he can't handle it himself.

5. His mother is his social companion in the evenings instead of his friends.

6. He is physically closer to his mother than to a girlfriend.

7. His anger keeps him trapped in situations that only his mother can resolve.

I told Trevor that it was not his fault that he had SIS. I said that it was doubtful he was born with the syndrome, but perhaps he had acquired it around the time his father left home. Pearl asked if she contributed to Trevor's disorder by depending on him for emotional security when her husband drank. I told her I didn't think so, because she had moved on with her life, whereas Trevor had not. I added that the only way to cure Trevor was to help him learn ways to be independent of his mother.

Both Trevor and Pearl were asked to record any behaviors that indicated Trevor was beginning to behave like a normal teenager. Any continuation of his old behavior would be confirmation of his SIS, and any independent functioning would be proof of his improvement.

Trevor's angry, oppositional behavior quickly decreased, and therapy was terminated a short while later. A follow-up after one year revealed no problems at school or with delinquent behavior. Pearl said that Trevor was much more social and had acquired a nice group of friends. She continued to date, although there still was no one signifi-cant in her life.

Trevor presented as an angry teenager who allowed no control in therapy. His mother, Pearl, was openly cooperative but powerless in light of Trevor's noncompliance. By exaggerating and reframing the presenting problem, Trevor's behavior became less oppositional and more independent. Pearl's attitude toward Trevor also evolved, from criticism to compassion to pride.

SYSTEMIC COMPENSATION SYNDROME

Jasmine was referred for therapy by another of my clients, a friend of Jasmine's mother. The 14-year-old girl had been to a series of nation-ally recognized eating disorder clinics with only marginal improve-ment over the past year. At five feet, two inches tall, she weighed only 70 pounds. Her mother, Edith, worried severely about Jasmine and arranged her own life so that she was accessible whenever Jasmine needed her. Edith would sit by the telephone while Jasmine was at school in case one of the teachers needed to call her. She had spoken to the school officials at length about Jasmine's condition so they could immediately detect any change in her well-being. Edith believed that if she and everyone else in Jasmine's life helped enough, the anorexia would stop.

Jasmine's father had left the family two years earlier and had returned to his native Australia. Jasmine said she missed her father terribly and could not understand why he not only had left them, but the country as well. Jasmine's intellectually challenged older sister had been placed in a residential facility shortly before the father's flight, and Edith worried that Jasmine felt that everyone in her life was leaving her.

Jasmine and Edith attended the first session together. During the initial phase of the appointment, Edith talked freely, but Jasmine hardly spoke. Any questions were greeted with silence or sneers. Edith suggested that Jasmine might feel more comfortable talking to me without her there, so she went to the waiting room. When her mother left the room, Jasmine was initially quiet, but then began madly shouting that while she had agreed to come to therapy, she couldn't go through with it. I empathized with Jasmine, agreeing that she had been through a lot lately and must be tired of talking about it to so many therapists. I suggested that we talk about other things, such as her passion for clothes, her friends, the trip she had recently taken. In a cold, confrontational tone, Jasmine said that she could not talk to me about anything. After 20 more minutes of attempts, I brought her mother back to the room.

I explained the situation to Edith, describing Jasmine's reluctance to communicate. Jasmine became hysterical, pointing at me and shrieking, "It's him, it's him, I can't talk because of him." She refused to tell her mother what it was about me, my appearance, or my demeanor that was so upsetting. Edith took her out to the car and then returned to express concern about Jasmine's behavior. In reality, she wanted to know what I had done to upset the girl so severely. I explained that I had only been complicitious, and there was no obvious explanation for why Jasmine had become hysterical.

Edith said that she tried to make every aspect of Jasmine's life as perfect as possible to avoid upsetting her. She let Jasmine determine what and where they ate, the television shows they watched, the clothes they both wore. I pointed out that Jasmine's anorexia seemed to have taken over Edith's life too. She agreed but stated that there was no other way of dealing with the problem.

Jasmine attended the second session only because she had promised her mother she would. She said she had not weighed herself recently but was certain she had gained some weight. From the drawn appearance of her face, I was not so sure. Jasmine sat and glared at me while her mother spoke. Her look was so contemptuous that even Edith felt sorry for me. As in the first session, Edith then left Jasmine alone with me. After several futile attempts to engage Jasmine in conversation, I decided to use the negative diagnosis approach. I told Jasmine that her anorexia was actually a symptom of another syndrome, that she was suffering from Systemic Compensation Syndrome (SCS). Jasmine coldly asked me what that was. I explained that her inability to eat or enjoy herself socially was related to her mother's insistence on being enmeshed in Jasmine's life. Because her mother refused to go out or have her own friends, Jasmine was unable to eat. Jasmine told me I was crazy, that I didn't know what I was talking about. I responded that I was certain that she would never be able to eat properly until her mother found a life of her own, and that her anorexia was the systemic compensation for Edith's problems.

I asked her mother to return and described the syndrome to her, as well. Jasmine denied having the disorder, but Edith wasn't so sure. Jasmine said that she wanted to return to her previous therapist, and that she would talk to him and tell him why she wouldn't eat. I said it would be worth a try, but with SCS, I doubted whether any therapist could make a difference until her mother had a fuller life.

A follow-up phone call to Edith revealed that Jasmine did see her former therapist twice, but then decided to terminate with him also. Edith was despairing, but I told her that was typical of SCS, and that she should really consider becoming independent as a way to help her daughter. My client, who was a friend of the family, mentioned a short time later that Edith had started going out socially and that Jasmine was eating more naturally. A chance meeting with the pair at a shopping mall six months later found Edith employed and Jasmine at a normal weight for her height.

It is customary to employ a variety of strategies to coax a hostile adolescent into participating in therapy. When these fail, the therapist works with other family members, helping them with establishing rules and consequences for the teenager. However, the adolescent does not typically offer the family any more control than was given the therapist. In these extreme situations of no control, a more successful outcome is achieved by exaggerating the presenting problem, forming it into a negative diagnosis. The syndrome becomes the target of the clients' opposition, and they work toward resolving their difficulties themselves. By rebelling against the therapist's perception and diagnosis of them, they are able to break their old patterns of behavior.

6

OPPOSITIONAL HYPNOSIS

Traditional hypnosis relies on the cooperation of the subject during the session. The process runs smoothly when a subject willingly enters into a trance, accepts suggestions given at the unconscious level, and uses these to overcome any problems. Having a cooperative subject means that the hypnotist is able to use straightforward directives to ameliorate a wide range of complaints, in the same manner that a therapist utilizes an authoritarian stance with a total control client.

It has long been recognized (Haley, 1976; Gilligan, 1987), however, that many subjects who present for hypnosis appear unwilling, resistant, and even hostile to the idea of being hypnotized. Their defiant attitudes are often related to previous failed attempts at resolving their problems or a reluctance to relinquish control to a therapist. Erickson (1976) felt this resistance was related to the overall symptomatology that brought these clients to therapy in the first place.

Even though clients oppose hypnotic suggestions, they are often anxious to have their problems resolved. They differ from other no control clients in that they are not generally oppositional and often go through the motions of cooperating during most of the session. Within the context of the trance state and induction, however, they refuse to relinquish control to the therapist and are noncompliant with hypnotic suggestions. With these no control subjects, an alternative approach that utilizes their opposition without demanding compliance is more productive than traditional methods.

METHOD

The oppositional hypnosis technique encourages the subject to be both defiant and difficult. The hypnotist frames the induction in such a manner that the subject's resistance or rebellion pushes them into a trance state. Once trance is achieved, there is still no attempt to achieve compliance with the subject. The therapist continues to make suggestions in such a way that the subject's defiance will enable the subject to solve his or her problems.

This technique is best used in the second session, after the hypnotist has been unable to elicit a trance state during the first meeting. It is often better to "fail" the first session, as difficult clients need to prove to the therapist how hopeless their situation really is. By initially giving clients a forum in which they can detail the immensity of their problems and complain about the unlikelihood that hypnosis will be able to rectify them, clients are better positioned to benefit from the oppositional hypnosis technique. Waiting until the second session also gives the hypnotist the opportunity to try a traditional induction and observe a client's typical pattern of responding.

For the oppositional hypnosis method to be effective, the subject must have been unable to follow basic hypnotic suggestions, such as closing the eyes, taking a deep breath, or responding to the hypnotist with a requested response. The hypnotist then reframes the suggestions, so that by defying them the subject enters into a trance. For example, if a subject refuses to close his or her eyes, the hypnotist suggests that an even deeper trance state can be reached by keeping the eyes open. The session is structured so that either cooperation or opposition leads to induction. Once hypnosis has been achieved, the therapist continues to give the subject instructions to rebel against, often asking the person to experience the presenting symptom rather than alleviate it. As the client opposes the suggestion, he or she gains control over the problem.

In this chapter, four cases are presented in which traditional and then oppositional hypnosis techniques were employed. By using redirection and an exaggeration of the presenting problem with these no control clients, a successful therapeutic outcome was achieved.

JOE'S DENTURES

Joe was referred for hypnosis by his dentist because he had a reflex gagging problem while being fitted for dentures. His difficulties had begun two years earlier when another dentist had determined that he needed a dental prosthetic. Since that time, Joe had been to six different dentists and had spent $7,000 without anyone being able to fit him with an upper denture. His current dentist felt that hypnosis might help.

Joe did not appear enthusiastic when he walked into my office. His first comment was that while he didn't feel he could be hypnotized, I might as well try anyway and join the list of those who had wasted his time and money. I asked Joe if he would rather consider psychotherapy since he didn't put any faith in the hypnosis. Joe laughed and said that the problem was in his mouth, not his head. He didn't have any problems except his inability to wear dentures. He then put his feet up on my desk and sipped on a can of soda.

I asked Joe why he wanted to solve his gagging problem. He patted his rather rotund stomach and said that life hadn't been worth living since he couldn't chew a good piece of steak. Everything about the dentures made him gag—the glue that held them, the plastic frame, the fitting process. He couldn't even stand to put a toothbrush in his mouth anymore. At 42 years of age, he didn't want to look like a toothless old man, and he knew that smiling with dentures was much more attractive than grinning with no upper teeth.

As we talked, Joe began to get irritated and finally told me to quit asking questions and to just hypnotize him. I tested him for suggestibility using the Spiegel eye roll technique. Joe refused to try and suggested that the whole entire session was futile. I checked for hand levitation, catalepsy of his arm, and progressive relaxation, all without success. I attempted hypnosis anyway, suggesting that Joe close his eyes and just listen. I gave Joe a set of direct suggestions commonly used in gagging situations. I told him that his new denture was gagging him because it felt bulky and strange, but that as I spoke, those sensations would slowly disappear. After he opened his eyes, his denture would feel comfortable and familiar, and he would not need to gag anymore.

When I asked Joe to open his eyes, he scowled at me and stated that the hypnosis had been a failure. He hadn't been in a trance and remembered everything that I said. Joe said that he could have opened his eyes whenever he wanted, that the whole experience was a bunch of bull. In addition, he said he could tell that the gagging had not gone away. I told Joe that I would like to try a different method next week, and if it were not effective, I would refer him to another professional. Joe mumbled something about joining the group as he walked out of my office.

Joe appeared for the next session in much the same mood as the first. I agreed with him that the previous attempt had ended in failure and apologized for the waste of time and money. I suggested that Joe not put any pressure on himself to go into a trance at this session, but should fail to go into a trance with his conscious mind. I told him that his conscious mind was too strong to be fooled by any of this and didn't allow his unconscious mind to accept any stupid suggestions. Joe looked at me with a trace of chagrin and asked what he could do about it.

I instructed him to look at the place where the wall and ceiling meet in the corner. I explained to him that it did not matter if his eyes remained open because he wasn't going to be able to go into a trance anyway. I chatted with Joe about a mother and daughter who had come for hypnosis the night before. I told him that neither of them had as strong or intelligent a conscious mind as Joe, but they had a highly developed unconscious that allowed them to solve their problems with hypnosis. I embellished the story, punctuating it with repetitive phrases, all affirming Joe's inability to be hypnotized.

Joe's eyes closed approximately five minutes later, and he entered a profound trance. I continued to give him suggestions challenging his state, and he rebelled by going into a deeper trance. I told Joe that his right arm could not move since he wasn't in a trance. If he were in a trance state, his unconscious mind would push his right arm up until his hand was floating in the air. As his right arm began to rise, I reiterated that his hand would remain still until he could attain a trance state. I added that since Joe could not achieve such a state, he would be unable to perform certain tasks that other subjects enjoyed.

The next step was to use Joe's opposition to solve his gagging problem. I gave him the suggestion to feel the dentures in his mouth and concentrate on the way they made him gag. Joe ran his tongue around the imaginary dentures but did not gag. I said, "That's right, Joe, you can continue to gag if your conscious mind tells you to." I reminded Joe about the taste of a good steak and commiserated with him that he would never have the opportunity to eat it since the glue holding the dentures in his mouth would cause him to gag. Joe continued to move his tongue over his dentures, and even made small chewing motions without any evidence of gagging. I made the suggestion that Joe would remember everything that had happened, and his total recall would be evidence that he hadn't been in a trance.

Joe emerged from the trance state quite disoriented. He remembered that I had instructed him to look at a spot on the wall. Despite my protestations, Joe swore that a trance state had been attained. After making another appointment, he left the session fairly confused.

The hypnosis lasted two more sessions, with Joe continuing to respond in the same manner. He made an appointment with his dentist for a fitting, and the dentist reported that Joe had successfully worn his dentures home. Two years later, while I was speaking to the dentist about another case, he mentioned that Joe had recently undergone extensive work on his lower teeth without any evidence of gagging during the procedure and that he continued to do well with his dentures.

Joe's hesitation and lack of cooperation with regard to hypnosis prevented him from benefiting from direct instructions. By giving him permission to reject my suggestions on a conscious level, he was able to use his oppositional stance against his own symptoms.

FALLING DOWN ON THE JOB

Nate, a 45-year-old college professor, came for hypnosis because, over the past five years, he had been experiencing difficulty having and keeping an erection. Three years previously, he and his wife had separated. Throughout the 21 years of their marriage, she had constantly criticized him, and in the two years prior to their separation, she had begun to attack his sexual performance, belittling his prowess as a lover. Because of this, they were rarely intimate, and Nate said that he felt under such pressure on those infrequent occasions that he was unable to maintain an erection even if he could achieve one.

Since his separation from his wife, Nate had fallen in love with a beautiful, younger woman, Eve, who was a visiting lecturer at his university. They wanted to live together once his divorce was final, but he was worried about having a positive sex life with her. Nate said he had difficulty maintaining an erection during intercourse with Eve and problems reaching orgasm even if he did manage to achieve one.

Nate had investigated a variety of techniques to solve the problem. He tried a hormonal drug, for example, but since it was only intermittently effective, he stopped using it. Whereas his wife had been cruel about his difficulty, Eve was supportive and understanding. He worried that she would eventually grow tired of the situation, however, and leave him for a younger man who could satisfy her sexually.

Nate added that he often had difficulty concentrating on his lovemaking. During intercourse, he would think about problems at work, appointments he needed to make, or what was on his desk. He also thought about the situation with his ex-wife and about his son, who was having problems at school. It seemed that Nate would think about anything that would keep him from experiencing pleasure during sex.

My first attempts at hypnosis met with poor success. Nate felt that hypnosis was just "hocus-pocus" and didn't believe that a man of his rationality could be hypnotized. Despite his reluctance, I tried an induction. Nate wanted to cooperate but became restless and fidgety. Nevertheless, I continued, using a standard set of suggestions that focused on asking Nate to make his arm rigid and hard and then transferring the ideation to his penis. I suggested that if he could make his arm rigid, he could do the same for his penis, and his erections would be firm and hard whenever he wished. When we finished, Nate thanked me, but said that he was skeptical about the process. He said that he didn't believe in the unconscious and felt that nothing had happened during the session that could help him maintain an erection. He agreed to try again the following week.

During the second session, I shifted to an oppositional hypnosis approach. I told Nate to close his eyes, but not to worry about going into a trance, pointing out that he had a brilliant, powerful mind, so there was no sense in asking his conscious processes to stop. After telling Nate to concentrate on his breathing and to give up trying to become hypnotized, I observed a definite change of state. Once he was clearly in a trance, I suggested that Nate resist having an intimate, satisfying relationship with Eve. I implied that his ex-wife would be unhappy if he were able to give pleasure to another woman. Instead, Nate should concentrate on his work rather than sex, using that brilliant mind of his, and thus prevent himself from achieving pleasure and making his ex-wife unhappy. He should never have an orgasm, as his body would probably have difficulty adjusting to that much pleasure. After 45 minutes in the trance state, I had Nate open his eyes. He commented, as he had after the first session, that he didn't think he could be hypnotized, and wondered how the process could be effective when he didn't even have any memory of my suggestions. I told him not to worry about the hypnosis until the following session.

Nate had satisfactory, even pleasurable, sex with Eve that week. At the beginning of the following session, we chatted briefly about his improvement and hypnosis in general. I once again put him into a trance, suggesting that he need not have strong erections because of his immense work load and his loyalty to his ex-wife. Nate canceled the following session, saying that he and Eve were so thrilled with his progress that he didn't see a need to continue. Six months later, Nate brought his son, who was having problems at school, in for therapy. He mentioned after the session that he had experienced two instances of difficulty in maintaining an erection since he had last seen me, but when he thought about calling for an appointment, the problem disappeared.

In Nate's case, a traditional hypnosis method was useless because of his high level of rationality and enmeshment in the mental process. By flowing with his opposition and giving suggestions in the context of Nate's mental machinations, I was able to use his resistance to counter his own maladaptive thought patterns.

ALL IN THE FAMILY

Mike, a 33-year-old business executive, came to my office requesting help to stop smoking. He wanted me to use hypnosis but doubted the technique would work because he knew he didn't really want to stop. When I asked why he was even bothering to try, Mike said that his family was very anxious for him to quit. His wife complained that the house and car smelled of smoke. His four-year-old son's asthma was being aggravated by Mike's smoking, and his seven-year-old daughter constantly begged him to stop. Mike worried that if he developed lung cancer or emphysema, his family would suffer emotionally and financially. He was a devoted family man; his idea of a good time was taking the family to a movie or on a picnic. Mike had tried to quit many times, but the reality was that he enjoyed smoking tremendously and always gave in to the temptation. He said he didn't think that hypnosis could help him, but he was willing to try for the sake of his family.

I used a traditional hypnotic induction for the first session. Mike cooperated and entered into a trance. The suggestions focused on getting him to feel strong and in control of his smoking. I had him imagine how positive things could be once he stopped, as his family would be happy, he would be healthy, and he would have more energy in general. The session concluded with a visualization of Mike's throwing his cigarettes away for good, an affirmation of his desire to quit smoking and live a healthier life.

Mike was depressed when he returned for the second session. He had begun the week with good intentions and managed to stop smoking for one day. While at a meeting on the second day, he smelled the smoke from someone else's cigarette and then couldn't stop thinking about how much he wanted one for himself. He bummed a cigarette from a friend, vowing that it would be his last. By the next day, however, he was buying a pack for himself. Mike became defensive, saying that he worked hard, and if he wanted some pleasure, he should be able to have it. Mike didn't even know why he had returned for another session, because, he added, he realized last week that hypnosis couldn't stop him from doing something he really wanted to do.

I suggested that we try again, since he was there. As in the first session, Mike was easily induced into a trance state. I decided to use the oppositional hypnosis form of suggestions, however, since Mike's desire to smoke was keeping him from relinquishing control. I asked Mike to envision himself smoking a cigarette and pointed out that, since he had no control over stopping, he should succumb to the pleasure of the experience. Mike was to imagine each step of smoking, from start to finish, savoring every moment.

I then suggested that Mike focus on his family, acknowledging their complaints and distress, but telling them how important it was for him to smoke. He was to dismiss their objections as trivial in light of the pleasure he obtained from smoking. Fears of poor health, lack of energy, and financial ruin were to disappear in a plume of smoke from his cigarette.

Mike emerged from his trance fairly confused. I suggested that he call me in the future if he wanted further help. Mike phoned several months later. He said that he had no idea whether the hypnosis had been responsible, but he had stopped smoking. Mike had done quite a bit of soul searching after the sessions and realized that his family and his health were worth more to him than a cigarette. Stopping had come naturally at that point.

In this case, Mike's opposition came from his love of smoking. By using the devotion to his family as a hook and exaggerating his pleasure from cigarettes, Mike's problem was able to be addressed using hypnosis.

PEACEFUL EXIT

A local attorney contacted me with an unusual problem. He had received a call from the wife of a client, asking him to declare his client *non compos mentis* because the man was refusing to seek medical attention for a gangrenous leg. The attorney believed that Charles, a 78-year-old retired colonel, was mentally sound, but was refusing help because he was afraid of what the doctors would discover. Charles had taken to bed and would not get out. His wife and daughters attended to him—feeding him, giving him sponge baths, and so on—but were concerned that Charles was not getting the medical care he needed. They pleaded with him daily to consult a doctor, but he refused to do so. The attorney asked if I would contact the family and see if Charles would accept my services.

I first spoke with Charles' wife, Elizabeth, who corroborated the information given by the attorney. She said that Charles was a strong-willed man, used to having his way at home and at work. Since he retired, he had become fascinated with breeding rare birds, but he even refused Elizabeth's help on that project. She and her daughters could not persuade Charles to do anything. Elizabeth asked if I would consider hypnotizing Charles into seeking medical attention. I agreed that I would speak to him about the possibility.

I met with Charles in his bedroom, introducing myself and informing him of his wife and daughter's intentions for him. I told him I could see he was fully in control of his faculties and so must have an excellent reason for refusing medical care. Charles glared at me and said that while he wasn't interested in having me there, at least I was perceptive enough to realize that he was sane. I asked Charles if he could imagine any reason, other than being crazy, that people might have for refusing to see a doctor when they knew they needed care. Charles suggested that someone might behave like that to avoid hearing bad news. I asked him if he would allow me to hypnotize him, since I was already there, because going through the motions might keep his wife and daughters from pestering him about seeing a doctor. Charles agreed to let me try, but scoffed at the notion that I could hypnotize him into doing anything.

I elected to begin with the oppositional hypnosis approach, since I knew I was unlikely to have another chance with Charles. The following is an excerpt from my work with him.

> I know this is your house, and I don't belong here, but your wife and daughters insisted that I come to help you with your health. I don't know who they think they are, telling either of us what to do, especially since you're the head of your family. You've always been in charge of them and are used to giving orders. All I know is that if someone asks you to help, it's important to try. There's nothing you have to do. You know that you can't be hypnotized, and you know you don't care what I have to say. You don't even have to listen to me with your conscious mind. Just act and breathe normally while you listen to my voice.

Charles' breathing became significantly heavier. He closed his eyes, and there was fluttering beneath the lids as he went into a light trance.

> I want to tell you a story. There was a bird that was wounded and couldn't fly. A man found the bird and wanted to help. The man was a magician and was anxious to try certain spells to heal the wound and make the bird fly again. The bird could not talk to the man so it was not sure how he could help. The magician soothed the bird

and assured it that he could understand it through its movements and by reading its mind. In this way, the magician would know which spells to try.

The session lasted for about 30 minutes, as the story was related in a soothing manner. Charles seemed relaxed at the end of the induction but ready for me to leave. I spoke briefly with the family before I departed and asked them to contact me if they wanted any further help.

I received a phone call from Elizabeth four days later. For the first time in six months, Charles had left his bed after my visit and gone to take a shower. In the process, he slipped and fell, and an ambulance had to be called to take him to the hospital, where the doctors examined his leg and discovered that the gangrene was secondary to bone cancer. They estimated that Charles would die within the week. Elizabeth said that Charles seemed peaceful with the news and was using the time to tie up financial matters and say good-bye to his friends and family.

Oppositional hypnosis is a useful technique in situations in which a client's personality or control issues make the person unavailable for standard induction. As with other therapeutic strategies, direct hypnotic procedures should be attempted first, with a switch to the oppositional method if noncooperation is demonstrated. By changing to the oppositional hypnosis technique, the therapist encourages clients to hold onto their opinions and defiance and use them to overcome their problems.

7

SYNDROMES

One of the most difficult situations of "no control" is when a client presents for treatment under the aegis of a diagnosis. Clients who have been determined by another professional to have a psychiatric syndrome, whether schizophrenia or attention-deficit disorder, are often resistant to intervention during therapy. The diagnosis marks the behavior as fixed or unchangeable, a product of the client's pathology. Often his or her entire personhood is defined by the problem. The client, as well as others, begin to refer to the diagnosis—"My husband is a borderline" or "I'm bipolar"—as a concrete entity. By accepting the syndrome, the client also buys the symptomatology associated with the disorder. Any improvement in functioning, such as that attained by medication, is seen as outside the client's direct control. This creates a high level of difficulty when the client appears for therapy. The therapist is given no control, and the client also sees himself or herself as powerless. It is a situation in which only the syndrome, or medical intervention, can affect the outcome.

Once a syndrome has been assigned, everyone surrounding the client mobilizes to solidify the diagnosis. Medical staff, family members, and the community position themselves to validate the condition, fleshing out details and making them fit. I had the opportunity to observe this process when working as an admissions social worker. A 35-year-old man came into the hospital exhibiting violent behavior. Everything about his actions suggested he was in the throes of a paranoid schizophrenic episode. Once the psychiatrist on duty made the diagnosis, the behavior of both the staff and the family shifted. Hall nurses duly noted any incomprehensible mutterings, psychologists documented hallucinatory reactions, and the man's family provided relevant history, such as his recent interest in religion. Two days later, however, the patient's psychotic behavior stopped completely. Blood analyses revealed that he had been suffering from lead poisoning and not paranoia. Corroborating information supporting this new diagnosis was obtained from all support personnel. The shift of syndrome created a corollary change in how he was treated by everyone involved. It was a clear demonstration of how acceptance of a diagnosis creates certain expectations. Once a client or family member believes in a disorder, therapeutic effectiveness is severely hindered.

Systems of therapy have developed a number of solutions to deal with syndromes. Narrative therapists often attempt to fight the diagnosis. By asking such questions as "When did autism enter the family?" or "How has schizophrenia tricked you?", they externalize the syndrome and try to extricate the client from its framework. Therapists using a psychoeducational approach accept the diagnosis and support the family as they function within its boundaries. Strategic therapy normalizes the diagnosis by removing its pathological connotations and redefines the problem as a product of its context. Therapists operating within a medical model reify the diagnosis, making the syndrome into a tangible, concrete entity that has prescribed treatment procedures, such as psychotropic medication or electroconvulsive therapy.

Other therapists reframe the disorders into something positive. This is an adaptation of the position taken in societies that view hallucinatory or erratic behavior as evidence of spiritual promise or shamanic power. Individuals who would be diagnosed as schizophrenic within our society instead are conceptualized as powerful beings possessing gifts that enable them to travel an alternative, inner path. Therapists who utilize this technique help their clients move from being debilitated by a condition to having value within a community.

Transpositional therapy views clients with previously diagnosed syndromes as an instance of no control, because their belief in their syndromes often prevents them from trusting the therapeutic process. As with other no control situations, the motivation for participating in therapy comes from creating a hook powerful enough to invest the client into the process without eliciting resistance. A therapist can be successful with these cases by accepting or exaggerating the diagnostic category while redirecting the client's focus from an intrapsychic to an interpersonal framework. By providing a context in which the client experiences competence, the import of the diagnosis begins to fade, and control is returned to both client and therapist by the end of treatment.

METHOD

Before utilizing the transpositional approach for clients offering no control because of a previously diagnosed condition, the following precursors should be observed.

1. The client has been determined by a professional as having a psychiatric illness. Obviously, the greater the stature of the diagnostician, the more impact the diagnosis has.

2. The diagnosis has been accepted by the client and/or a significant family member.

3. The diagnosis is seen as negative and inevitable. This technique would not be useful in cultural contexts that frame the syndrome as positive, such as a shamanic gift, or view it as a temporary, insignificant problem.

4. Despite the syndrome, the client has appeared in therapy for help with a problem, either individually or as part of a family group.

5. The therapist is given latitude to address the issue, without interference from either the professional who made the diagnosis or the one who is managing the case medically. Obviously, any negative input from either of these sources would further limit the control of the therapist.

The treatment strategy focuses on accepting the diagnosis to the point of ignoring it. Therapy is redirected to other interpersonal issues that have sufficient power to invest the client in change. Once the client is able to act independently and productively within the context of the disorder, the syndrome diminishes in importance. In the following section, three cases are presented to illustrate the technique.

ALL MY CHILDREN

Dan, a 42-year-old recently diagnosed bipolar, was referred for family therapy by a community medical care team because his children were having problems. Dan's history of erratic emotional functioning had created a number of difficulties for his four children. The team's hope was that I could help the children cope more effectively in light of their father's disorder.

Claire, Dan's wife, had asked him to leave the family home six months earlier. During the 20 years of their marriage, Dan had wreaked havoc with their finances—spending their savings, stealing from his children, and entering into risky business ventures without consulting Claire. When Dan began an affair with the wife of her boss, Claire decided she had endured enough. She said she believed that Dan's behavior was a product of his illness, but that she could not cope with him anymore.

The four children—Albert, age 19; Bill, age 17; Victor, age 15; and Lydia, age 8—said they loved their father very much and forgave him for his transgressions. After the medical team explained their father's illness to them, they felt Dan was not responsible for his actions.

Dan agreed to attend therapy, even though he was not certain what he could accomplish because of his condition. He did not think his current medications were stabilizing him properly. He had recently stopped working as a jeweler because his customers were complaining about his unreliability. Dan wanted desperately to return home and was anxious for his wife to accept him back.

Everyone was weepy during the first session. The children described how Dan's manic behavior frightened them, especially when he was driving. Two of the boys, Victor and Bill, were protective of their father. They said they remembered him as a loving, dedicated father before the illness took hold. The boys talked about how much time their father had devoted to them when they were little, and how he had later taught them the jewelry craft. Albert, the oldest boy, saw his father as defective, and was angry that Dan was unavailable. Since the age of 12, he had assumed his father's role as anchor and protector of the family. Lydia, the youngest child, seemed detached from Dan. She did not remember much of her father prior to the exacerbation of his illness, and Dan had never shown much interest in her because of his depression. Lydia sat on her mother's lap for most of the session and rarely looked in her father's direction.

Dan said that his primary motivation for attending with the family was to reconcile with Claire. He was currently living with friends and collecting disability payments. He said there were times when he missed his wife so much that he felt suicidal. Claire's attitude was ambivalent during Dan's discourse. She said that she still loved her husband and felt sorry for him, but was angry at the way he had disrupted the family. Claire maintained that her primary responsibility was to her children. She worried about the effect Dan's illness would have on their development and feared that one of her children would grow up to be like their father.

The subsequent session was much like the first. Dan begged his wife to let him return; Claire attacked Dan's history of misconduct, while excusing him because of his illness; the oldest son blamed his father for disrupting the family and leaving his mother alone; the two middle boys cried for Dan and asked him to spend time with them; and the girl ignored her father. Except for Lydia, it appeared that everyone in the family wanted someone who was unavailable to them.

It became obvious that whenever I would make a suggestion, Claire would discount it, saying that nothing would work because of Dan's illness. She refused to believe that Dan could improve or change. I concurred with Claire, but reminded her that the family was referred for therapy to address difficulties the children were having. Therefore, they, and not Dan, should be the focus of our attention.

I suggested that the two middle boys, Bill and Victor, were depressed because no one responded to their requests to be with their father. If they wanted to spend time with Dan, they should be allowed to do so in a safe situation, even if Claire felt it was a mistake in light of Dan's bipolar condition. Their father's involvement with Bill and Victor would also give Albert some freedom in relation to his brothers.

Over the next several sessions, Dan was encouraged to become more active with his children. He helped Bill and Victor with their jewelry making and went to watch all of the children when they participated in sports. Gradually, Dan became more focused and less depressed. He abandoned the idea of winning Claire back and was happy to connect with her through the children.

A follow-up one year later found Claire and Dan divorced. It was actually Dan who decided to terminate the marriage; Claire had been reluctant to make the split final. Dan continued to see his children on a regular basis and was employed as a jeweler. Claire was working at a job she enjoys and reported that the children had no major problems.

By shifting the focus away from Dan's disorder and onto other interpersonal relationships within the family, sufficient control was obtained to effect change. The syndrome became incidental to other issues, allowing the family to participate in therapy and to give control to the therapist.

THE LOVE OF JESUS

Paranoid schizophrenics have prominent delusions that can be persecutory or grandiose in nature, frequently following a particular theme. Individuals with this disorder can display anxious, fearful, or argumentative behavior, especially if their delusions are not believed by the therapist. In addition, because schizophrenia is typically treated within the context of a medical model, therapy is often devalued because it is seen as outside the "real" treatment of medication, education, and hospitalization. Families who appear for help often give the therapist no control simply because they cannot conceptualize how therapy could be effective with an organic condition.

The Davis family appeared for therapy because the son, Larry, was refusing to take his medication. Larry had been diagnosed as paranoid schizophrenic by a number of mental health clinics over the past few years. He was prescribed a variety of psychotropic medications, but he no longer wished to take them, claiming that the drugs made him feel angry. As Larry believed he was an incarnation of Jesus Christ, such negative emotions interfered with his calling to be loving and caring.

Larry's mother, Mrs. Davis, was anxious that he reinstate his medications. She said she doubted therapy would be useful with her schizophrenic son, but as Larry refused to see his doctor, she felt it would be better than doing nothing at all. Mrs. Davis had devoted herself to her son's care, a role she carried alone, since Mr. Davis spent long hours at work and never made time for Larry. She was concerned that if Larry did not go back to the clinic soon, he would enter a more serious phase of the illness and be even less functional.

Mr. Davis believed Larry should make his own decisions. He accepted the psychiatric diagnosis but felt that his son should be able to live life as he chose. If Larry wanted to stand on street corners with his long hair and white robe and preach to people, he said, that should be his privilege.

Larry alternated between living with his parents and staying with his girlfriend and his four-year-old son. Most of the time, he believed he was Jesus Christ, but there were moments when he wasn't sure. I asked Larry what made him doubt who he was. He said that when he was a burden to his family and friends, he didn't feel much like Jesus.

I asked Larry's parents to estimate how much money they had spent to meet his expenses over the past year. Mrs. Davis said that it was probably close to $30,000, but that the amount was immaterial, since Larry was sick and needed their help. I suggested that, since Larry was refusing to take his medicine, the money might be better allocated as a salary for him. Mr. and Mrs. Davis could pay Larry the $30,000 so that he could fulfill his mission as Jesus. Larry would be able to utilize his time doing good deeds and caring for others. In particular, since Mr. Davis was a busy man who needed to spend his time earning a living, Larry could attend to Mrs. Davis' needs for social stimulation. Larry would actually be employed by his father to escort his mother to the theater, to see long absent friends, and to take walks in the park. Mrs. Davis wouldn't need to complain about her husband's long working hours, because she would have her son as a paid companion. Larry could meet his calling by filling a void in his mother's life.

Mrs. Davis said the idea was preposterous, that she was perfectly capable of looking after herself, and certainly didn't need her schizophrenic son to entertain her. Mr. Davis thought it was a fine idea; Larry would be gainfully employed, and his wife would stop complaining about how much time he spent at the office. Larry wasn't sure about the whole thing.

Only Larry and his mother returned for the next session. Mrs. Davis informed me that she had spent most of the week visiting an old friend, which showed that she was perfectly capable of looking after herself. In her absence, Larry had stayed with his girlfriend and son. He also had a job interview later that week. I suggested that Larry be very cautious about finding work. Because he was schizophrenic, Larry needed to be dependent on his family. Besides, his illness could prevent him from being successful at his job, and if he were going to convince people he was Jesus Christ, he needed to be infallible. Mrs. Davis commented that perhaps I needed to see one of Larry's psychiatrists.

Larry came to the next session by himself. He told me he got the job and was beginning work the next day. His mother had convinced him she didn't need his help, so Larry felt he would be more useful somewhere else. He was moving in with his girlfriend to care for her and his son. Larry said he liked me a lot, but he would be unable to continue therapy since his work would occupy so much of his time.

A follow-up a year later found Larry still living with his girlfriend and son. His girlfriend said she enjoyed Larry's taking a more productive role in the family. Larry has kept his job and was still off medication. A phone call to Mr. and Mrs. Davis found them doing fine. Mrs. Davis indicated that she heard from Larry only occasionally and suggested I call him if I wanted to know how he was doing.

In this case, an exaggeration of the syndrome in the context of the family's interpersonal relationships enabled them to resolve their problems. A paradoxical approach, rather than direct intervention, was more practical in this situation of no control.

MAN OF THE HOUR

Teddy, age 13 was referred to therapy by the psychologist at his special school. Teddy had been diagnosed with Pervasive Developmental Disorder (PDD). He was very bright, but his syndrome had resulted in behavior that was disrupting his family. Teddy's father, Martin, was consumed by Teddy's problems and found it difficult to move beyond them in his relationship with his son. Teddy's mother, Pauline, seemed unaffected by his behavior and constantly berated her husband for paying attention to it.

During the first session, Martin recited the details of Teddy's problem as if he were quoting from the DSM-IV. He highlighted Teddy's difficulties with his peers, his inability to inhibit talking about specific topics, and his inappropriate silliness. Teddy was overly affectionate, even to strangers, and his memory for details was phenomenal. Pauline interrupted to tease Martin, saying that his recall of the fine points of Teddy's behavior was exceptional itself. Pauline said her son's actions were typical of those of any growing boy. Teddy's behavior didn't upset Pauline, no matter how much her husband worried. Martin suggested to his wife that Teddy's need to be in a special school might be evidence that something was wrong with the boy.

Pauline complained that Martin spent a good deal of time trying to fix Teddy's problem. She was left to handle the rest of the family issues, so they had little time together as a couple. Whenever they tried even to have a conversation, Teddy would interrupt by acting silly. I commented that an inability to inhibit behavior was a key feature of PDD. I suggested that we might use another aspect of the syndrome, the focus on routine, to alleviate some of the difficulty.

I asked the family to let Teddy be "on stage" from 7:00 to 7:30 every evening. At this time, he was allowed to perform for the family. He could be silly, show off his memory for details, or ask his parents questions. At any other point during the day or evening, when Teddy tried to act silly with his parents, he would be told to save it for "Teddy time."

The family agreed to try. When they returned the next week, they reported that the intervention had been a success. Teddy would entertain his parents for a half hour each evening, and the sillier he became, the more they would applaud. Martin pointed out that the sessions were even educational, since Teddy's knowledge of geography was astounding. Teddy loved being on stage, and his parents liked having a time when they didn't have to correct him or argue with each other about his behavior.

Martin began to enjoy Teddy more and worry about him less. He enrolled both of them in karate classes. Teddy was initially very timid, but the instructor was patient and managed Teddy well within the class. Martin enjoyed being able to talk to his son about a common interest, and Teddy was soon impressing his classmates with information he culled about the martial arts.

Pauline and Martin began to spend more time together, and even arranged to stay for a night in a motel for their anniversary. Martin was more understanding about Pauline's desire to enjoy Teddy without correcting him, and Pauline became firmer and more helpful to her son.

8

THE SINS OF THE SIBLINGS: THE USE OF PENANCE IN FAMILY THERAPY

There are times in therapy when a client appears anxious to resolve a problem, but because of personality qualities or underlying issues is unable to commit to the process. Direct suggestions by the therapist are partially or unenthusiastically carried out. The client gives enough control to the therapist to make sessions run smoothly, but resolution of the problem is never achieved. Historically, in these partial control situations, both the therapist and the client become frustrated, each blaming the other for lack of progress.

As mentioned in Chapter 1, it is more productive in interactions of partial control to uncover a hook that is powerful enough to invest the client fully into the therapeutic process. These strong hooks are generally found within the underlying problems, rather than in the presenting issues. The hook and tool selected by the therapist must be potent enough to motivate the client, but not so intimidating that the client becomes resistant.

The underlying factors related to problems of adult clients often lie within the context of their family of origin, even if they are grown with families of their own. Therapists typically focus on the adult client's parents as the cause of distress, particularly on the trauma they may have promoted during the client's childhood. However, the dynamics of the issue may also be connected to the client's relationships with siblings, since clients often carry their status within their family of origin into future interactions. As children, siblings finesse for position within the family structure. This struggle persists into adulthood, since whether the client was the favored or the dismissed child, and whether the client had to fight his or her brothers and sisters for affection from their parents, can affect the client's later behavior.

Adults often feel uncomfortable admitting that these early difficulties are still upsetting them. They strive to use adult coping mechanisms—tolerance, removing themselves from contentious situations, discourse—to deal with the problem. Even in situations where family members live at a considerable distance from each other and barely communicate, a client's behavior can be affected by previously disruptive emotional bonds. Because of this, the client's relationship with siblings is often a powerful enough hook to motivate the client to resolve the presenting problem. The technique described in this chapter focuses on how to use such underlying issues to work with partial-control clients.

METHOD

The concept of penance has been used extensively in religious contexts. In penance, the individual voluntarily performs some act of self-mortification to show remorse for wrongdoing. This act of contrition is supposed to free the participant through the acceptance and subsequent absolution of the misdeed. Penance should be differentiated from reparation or restitution, which involve making amends to the victim of an affront or a crime. Although both processes make the participant responsible for past actions, penance can be used in situations where the client themselves is the victim. The act of penance generates sufficient power to help the client resolve the problems and acquire a more positive reframing of his or her relationship with the perpetrator.

The technique is best used when the following conditions exist.

1. Direct attempts to resolve the client's problems have met with an impasse. The client wants to overcome the problem, but lacks the motivation or ability to accomplish tasks.

2. The underlying problem is linked to the client's inability to resolve the issues. The client has indicated that his or her rela-

tionship with another person is responsible for the client's current state, or the client sees himself or herself as a victim of another person's behavior.

3. The hook and tool developed have enough emotional intensity to invest the client into carrying out the plan.

4. The therapist can envision the technique's leading to a positive outcome.

5. The client understands the purpose of the intervention is to resolve the problem.

Once committed to this method, the therapist continues to use the same intervention at subsequent sessions. Details about the execution of the strategy and its success are obtained at each meeting. Together with the client, the therapist alters or intensifies the directive to make the plan more palatable or effective. The therapist abandons the intervention only when it clearly is not working or is causing the client too much distress.

In the following sections, the technique of penance is applied to three cases involving siblings. While the strategies used are similar, the form of the intervention is modified to meet the needs of the individual client. It should also be noted that in all three cases, the technique can be used even though the relevant family member does not participate in therapy.

COCAINE

At the age of 32, Ray appeared to have the world by the tail. He had turned his father's small construction business into a multimillion dollar enterprise. He drove a Corvette to work each day and lived in a six-bedroom house. Ray was married to his high school sweetheart, Cathy, and he described his relationship with his wife as loving and supportive. The couple and their two attractive, intelligent children presented as a picture-book family—except for the fact that every two weeks Ray would binge on cocaine.

When Ray's brother, Barry, invited him three years earlier to try cocaine, Ray accepted out of curiosity. In the beginning, Ray snorted cocaine about once a month. As the two brothers began to use together, Ray became addicted and began injecting cocaine every two weeks. Barry ended up in prison on dealing charges, and Ray tried to obtain the help of a drug counselor. He managed to stay drugfree for seven months, but then started using again.

Ray always returned from his binges feeling depressed and ashamed. To avoid the expected confrontation with Cathy, he would stay in a motel for two days, too ashamed to deal with his family. He would then return home, promising never to use cocaine again. Cathy would forgive him, and he'd stay clean until the next time.

When the couple appeared for the first session, Ray had recently returned from a cocaine binge. When he came home this time, Cathy was so angry that she smashed Ray's car with a baseball bat. Both Ray and Cathy wanted to resolve the problem before their marriage and life collapsed.

I asked Ray about his family history. He reported a difficult relationship with his parents, particularly his mother. Ray said his mother spent all of her time complaining. After selling his construction business to Ray, the father developed a successful chain of gas stations. Ray commented that his relationship with his father had always been distant, and that he rarely spoke with either parent, even though they live only a block from his house. Ray refused to consider bringing his parents into therapy with him.

When asked about his brother, Barry, Ray broke into tears. He said he was furious with his brother for introducing him to cocaine. To make matters worse, now that Barry was in prison and clean by necessity, he would lecture Ray on the evils of cocaine whenever Ray visited him. Ray was angry at the idea that Barry, an inmate, was instructing him, but he could never argue with his brother because he knew that Barry was right. He chose to avoid the whole scene by no longer visiting his brother in prison. Ray complained that Barry had always been treated better by their parents, and even though he was in jail, his mother still held Barry up to Ray as an example. She excused Barry's behavior and always spoke lovingly when discussing him with Ray. Ray suggested that perhaps if he went to prison, his mother would be nicer to him.

Therapy initially attempted to use the positive marital relationship to stop Ray's bingeing. Despite his good intentions, however, Ray was still using cocaine. I made the decision that a more powerful hook was required, one that would invest Ray into the therapeutic process. I explained to Ray that his brother was responsible for starting him on cocaine. But despite that past mistake, Barry was now working hard to make sure that Ray didn't end up in prison as well. I suggested that from now on, every time Ray used cocaine, he was to visit Barry in jail. Cathy would drive him there. When Barry lectured him on the evils of cocaine, Ray was to write down every word. At the end of the visit, Ray was to thank his brother and promise to do better. After Cathy brought him home, Ray would call his parents and tell them how helpful Barry had been.

Ray and Cathy agreed to the assignment. Two weeks later, when Ray went on a cocaine binge, Cathy took him to the prison as planned, and Ray listened to Barry's lecture. Ray commented that Barry had been very surprised to see him there, and was even more startled when Ray thanked him for the lecture. Cathy said that Ray was teary when he returned to the car, but didn't give her any of the details of the emotional visit.

Therapy continued for two more months, although Ray never binged again. The couple asked to work on child-rearing issues, and their 12-year-old daughter was involved in the sessions, because Cathy was worried that the girl had many of the addictive personality traits of her father. The therapy terminated with the understanding that Ray and Cathy would contact me if any relapse occurred.

A follow-up 18 months later revealed that Ray was still clean. He had voluntarily visited Barry two more times in jail. His brother was now free and planning to get married. Ray said that he didn't particularly like the woman, but he was comfortable with letting Barry make his own decisions and planned to be in the wedding.

The technique used in this case involved constructing a "penance" for Ray's cocaine use. Because the intervention was linked to the underlying issues involving his brother, it was sufficiently noxious and powerful to invest Ray into changing his presenting problem.

SARCOIDOSIS

Mary, age 28, was referred for therapy by her physician, because she was suffering from sarcoidosis, a lung disease with no known cure. Her physician believed Mary's symptoms were of psychological rather than physiological origin. Mary had recently left her clerical job because of stress caused by her illness. She frequently experienced pain on her left side, particularly around her chest. Headaches flared up at the slightest provocation. She felt depressed all the time and cried easily, spending most of her day in bed waiting for the pain to subside. She agreed to come to therapy because she wanted desperately to return to work.

Mary currently lived with her fiancé and her two children. Her two brothers, Mickey, age 25, and William, age 27, and William's wife resided in the house as well. Mickey worked as a carpenter when he wasn't drunk. William and his wife were heroin addicts and unemployed, although Mary suspected that William's wife worked as a prostitute to earn drug money. Mary had one sister, Dorie, age 24, who was a crack addict and lived on the streets. The only sibling who was not a user was Bobby, age 26, who was a lab technician and had his own apartment.

Mary's parents had been separated for two years. Her father was an alcoholic who worked at a local plant as a laborer. Her mother was a licensed practical nurse employed in a hospital. Mary saw herself as being much like her mother, and she felt close to her even though they rarely visited each other. Mary felt the level of stress in her life had increased significantly when her parents split and her brothers came to stay with her.

As Mary discussed her brothers' arrival, the pain in her neck and chest area intensified. The sensation continued until I changed the topic. It was clear that her symptomatology was linked to her siblings, and if they could exacerbate the pain, they should be useful in ameliorating the problem.

The initial phase of therapy centered on directing Mary in ways in which she could take better care of herself, an approach that was highly unsuccessful. She wanted to lose her symptoms, but the overwhelming home situation precluded her from being strong enough to do so. A hook was needed to provide the impetus for her to achieve control.

I suggested to Mary that perhaps she was using the pain to keep from caring for her brothers properly. She needed to be more like her mother, a woman who devoted herself to caring for sick people. Mary's brothers had serious alcohol and drug addictions that precluded them from leading a normal life, and they desperately required her assistance. Every time Mary experienced pain, she should see it as a signal that she needed to help her brothers more. I told her that she should make sure that they had nourishing meals and should comfort them if they were distressed. She could collect information about helping them with their addictions and take them to appropriate agencies. Now that Mary wasn't working, she would have time to devote to her brothers' care. She might even consider emulating her mother and study nursing, so that she could care for her brothers better. In any event, Mary should view her pain as a warning that she needed to do more for her brothers.

Mary disliked the suggestion intensely. She said she felt she needed to spend her time helping her fiancé and children rather than her brothers. I asked her to spend two weeks trying my idea before she dismissed it. By the end of the month, Mary had thrown her brothers out of the house. She sent Mickey to a detoxification center and William and his wife to a special program for drug addicts. Her fiancé, who used to drink with Mickey, was told he could remain with her as long as he stayed sober. Mary enrolled in a special employment program for low-income families and began training as a nurse's assistant. Therapy continued for another two months.

A six-month follow-up revealed that Mary had completed her nursing program, despite a 75 percent dropout rate overall, and was working in a clinic as an intern. She and her fiancé had finally set a wedding date, and she was still painfree. Her brothers had relapsed from their treatment program and returned home. After a week, she again asked them to leave, informing them she needed her own life and could no longer care for them.

The penance suggested to Mary was so offensive that she rebelled and took charge of the situation and her pain. Only by the use of such a powerful hook was she able to make the changes she needed in her life.

BULIMIA

Janice, age 24, entered therapy to resolve her purging problem. She was attractively slim, but was highly depressed because she believed she was overweight. She was also disturbed by the measures she took to correct the situation. Janice's demeanor was very sociable and pleasant. She said she took great pains to hide her bulimia from others. She enjoyed her job in a stylish boutique and the opportunity it gave her to obtain all the latest fashions. Janice and her husband, Jim, had been married for six years, and while he knew about her purging, it didn't concern him.

Janice openly discussed her problem and her family history during the first session. She mentioned that she had three sisters, one older and two younger than she. Her parents had divorced 11 years previously, and Janice's youngest sister still lived with her father while attending college. Janice said she rarely saw them because married life kept her too busy. Her mother had remarried an obnoxious man and lived with him in the Midwest. Janice said her mother called several times a week, primarily to complain about her life and her marriage. Janice's older sister, who was also in college, had a physical disability that had made her very unhappy when she was growing up, and she still tended to be unpleasant.

Janice's sisters knew about her bulimia and were very nice to her when she was purging, in contrast to their demands for help when she was not bingeing. They constantly asked her for assistance with their problems, but whenever she tried to help, they were critical of her attempts. Janice felt that her purging was a means of keeping her sisters "off her back." Whenever she was bulimic, her sisters became compassionate and stopped their whining. Janice believed she had the same reaction to her mother's telephone calls.

The first three months of therapy were marginally successful in solving Janice's bulimia. After one intense session, Jim announced that he'd had enough. Janice's bulimia was not his problem, and he didn't want to attend any more therapy. After Jim's exit, I felt that Janice's best chance for success in individual therapy would be to include the rest of her family, even if on a covert level.

I told Janice that she would have to work even harder to conquer her problem since her husband was no longer participating. I asked her to list everything she ate when bingeing, and she wrote down the various junk foods she used. Janice also mentioned that any evening when she planned to purge, she would put a slice of butter on her food at dinner. She would then pick a fight with Jim so that he'd leave her alone, and go upstairs where he couldn't hear what she was doing. After turning on the hot and cold water faucets, Janice would don a gray sweatsuit in preparation for vomiting.

Because of the highly ritualistic nature of her behavior, I believed a similarly powerful intervention was needed. I asked Janice to carry out the following task.

1. Janice was to time her bingeing and purging from start to finish.

2. Every time she purged, she was to call each of her sisters and her mother and offer to help them in some way. If they refused her assistance, she was to insist, encouraging them to come up with some way she could help them. No demand was to be perceived as too difficult.

3. Whatever length of time Janice calculated in step 1 must be doubled for step 2. If her bingeing and purging took one hour, she must spend at least two hours helping her family.

4. Janice was to wear the same sweatsuit she used for purging when contacting her family. She was also to hold a stick of butter in her hand while she called them on the phone.

5. No one was to know the details of the task except the two of us.

Janice accumulated 12 hours of service to her family the first week because of six hours of bingeing and purging. After spending six hours helping her sisters, she called to complain she didn't know what else to do. I recommended that she call her mother and listen to her moaning. She could also take her lonely older sister to a dance and help her meet men. I suggested that Janice might clean the bathroom of her especially irritable sister, because doing so might brighten her sister's day enough to make her cheerful. Janice said she got the idea and hung up.

Janice binged and purged only twice the following week and spent approximately four hours helping her family. I expressed concern that her family must be feeling deprived, and Janice laughed. She did not have another episode that month. A follow-up one year later found Janice still free of bulimia.

Janice's penance invested her in the healing process and allowed her to accomplish her goal. In this case, as in the preceding ones, the underlying antagonistic relationships within the family were used to motivate the client. Penance removed the impasse of partial control and allowed the clients to reach their therapeutic goals, addressing both the presenting and underlying problems.

9

THE ART OF CHATTING

Historically, chatting was viewed as an adjunct of therapy, a means of exchanging pleasantries at the beginning of a session before the real "business" took place. In some therapeutic systems, chatting with a client was actually discouraged, as it was seen as being overly familiar and as compromising the professional demeanor of the therapist. Other orientations, such as psychoanalysis, viewed any conversational comments by the client as fraught with meaning and available for interpretation. If a patient noticed that there was fresh coffee in the waiting room and asked for a cup, the analyst would inquire why he or she would make such a request and direct the client toward discussing other unmet needs. Feeling-based systems often used chatting to connect with clients, a way of letting them know that the therapist was empathetic and available.

Chatting can be useful in making clients feel comfortable during therapy, especially since asking for help from a stranger in an unknown setting can be intimidating. Chatting normalizes the therapeutic environment and places it into the familiar context of social interaction. The therapist assumes human dimensions and is framed as someone who can be approached and who will listen.

Chatting can also be a potent therapeutic tool. An observant therapist can glean useful information from a chat. Clients often indicate areas of interest that can be used to hook them into interventions at a later time. An offhand discussion of a recent event, such as an office party or family wedding, can yield information about the client's feelings and interactions with others. A joke or story can form the foundation of shared experience, which is remembered long after other therapeutic interactions. Carl Whitaker used to tell how he took schizophrenic patients for a walk around town during boring sessions, and his clients commented that this was often the most significant part of the therapy for them.

Chatting is effectively used as a bridge when therapy reaches an impasse. Clients frequently withhold control from a therapist if issues become too sensitive, impending change seems threatening, or an aspect of their personality or culture prohibits their compliance. At these times, a therapist can reduce the level of anxiety within the session by shifting to a more conversational mode. Vulnerable or volatile issues are put on hold until the therapist can find an indirect approach more acceptable to the client. Often, the chat will simply relax the situation sufficiently for the client to confront the issues.

There is an art to chatting, an ability to put others at ease and allow them the freedom to be interesting. Some therapists are naturally sociable or playful. Others do not exhibit those qualities even in their personal life. It is important that therapists converse with clients in a way that is comfortable for them and not force the behavior. There is nothing more ridiculous, or ineffective, than a stiff, formal therapist attempting to be chatty and hip. Conversations that utilize the therapist's own natural social proclivities are more productive than are canned attempts at being warm and humorous.

Chatting is also capable of improving other therapeutic skills. While teaching a course on family therapy, I noticed that some students who were engaging and conversationally creative during normal interactions would become stiff automatons when role playing a therapist. By encouraging the students to chat with "clients" during their mock sessions, their demeanors and verbal expressions during the "working" part of the therapy also improved.

It is important to give clients clear signals as to when you are chatting and when you are in a more therapeutic mode. Body language, phrasing, and openness should change with the level of conversation. This shifting allows clients to understand what is expected of them in the interaction—when they are working, when they can relax. A skillful therapist can interject chatting into any phase of a session, using it to pace the therapeutic interaction.

DEVELOPMENTAL CHATTING

Chatting, as with other social interactions, needs to change as a function of the participants. One of the key factors in determining the form of the interchange is the developmental level of the participants. Chatting style should reflect the cognitive and social abilities of the recipients and the changing interests of clients as they age. A conversation about Ninja turtles would be as ridiculous with an elderly client as would a discussion of weather conditions with an infant. The following sections detail the relevant developmental and interest shifts related to chatting with a client.

Infant and Toddler Chatting

Infants are not normally great conversationalists, and even if they are the identified client, the infant is usually not the agent of change in the therapy. Toddlers often detract from adult interactions during therapy, as they zip around investigating every object in the office. The focus of the session frequently shifts to making sure that everyone and everything emerges from the meeting in one piece rather than helping the clients with their problems. These youngest members of the family, however, should not be viewed only as distractions, because they can be effectively used to engage other participants.

Infants are often accurate emotional barometers of the family climate. Their affective quality is usually indicative of the level of stress in the home. Since infants have no filter on their emotional responses, their reactions reveal aspects of home life without the dissimulation seen in older family members. Babies who cry incessantly, who appear lethargic, or who have difficulty eating and sleeping are frequently indicating there is a problem in the home environment.

Chatting with or about a baby can reveal how family members position themselves with regard to a number of other issues, as family dynamics are made clear in relation to the newest member. Coalitions appear, hierarchies become evident, and typical coping strategies are identified, simply by the therapists interacting with the baby in a playful manner. For a therapist who feels comfortable in doing so, sitting on the floor and playing with an infant can yield more information than will hours of clinical interviews.

Infants can also be useful entries to reluctant or antagonistic participants. Confrontation between couples will sometimes be defused when their child does something "cute." Clients who feel threatened by a therapist or who are apprehensive about therapy will often relax if the therapist plays with their baby.

Hank, a 15-year-old-boy, was referred for therapy by his divorced parents because he had threatened suicide four times in the past few weeks. Hank lived with his mother and a half-brother, six months old. Hank had previously seen another therapist after becoming depressed when his parents separated, but he refused to talk with that counselor again. During the initial phone call, it became apparent that Hank's father was furious at the permissiveness of the mother. She allowed Hank to have drinking buddies over during the week, and these friends often ended up spending the night at the house after passing out. Hank's father wanted his son to live with him so he could provide better supervision.

At the scheduled appointment time, Hank's mother came into my office, informing me that the boy refused to come inside. I decided to take the session to the car, where I found Hank, his father, and his infant brother, Jerome. After settling in, I tried unsuccessfully to engage Hank in conversation about his feelings, the suicide threats, or his parents' separation. I finally abandoned the questioning and began to play with Jerome. After a while, Hank joined in, and soon we were taking turns making Jerome laugh. With this base of rapport, I was able to reintroduce some of the family issues, and this time, Hank was willing to talk. By the end of the session, Hank had agreed to live with his father for the next month. His mother concurred as long as it wouldn't affect her child support payments. A deal was struck between the parents to handle the finances. By establishing rapport with his baby brother, I was able to reduce Hank's resistance and resolve the initial crisis.

Childhood Chatting

Preschool and school-age children are much more proficient chatters than are their infant counterparts. Sometimes, however, a young child is shy in the presence of a strange adult and so is reluctant to talk. If direct questions or playing with a toy fails to engage the child, the therapist should chat with an adult or other family member instead of pursuing the interaction with the youngster. The more relaxed the interaction with a parent or sibling, the sooner the child will accept the therapist as a safe adult.

> Four-year-old Marie was referred to the clinic because of horrible nightmares. She frequently woke at night screaming. Her mother was at a loss as to what was causing such terrifying dreams as the family situation was relatively stable. After entering the office, Marie clung to her mother's leg, and every attempt at conversation resulted in the girl's burrowing her face in her mother's skirt. I tried to entice Marie with a doll, paper and crayons, and wind-up toys. Nothing worked. Finally, I began to chat with Marie's mother about the wallpaper we had recently installed in the office. For ten minutes we talked about colors, patterns, and the quality of the workmanship. By the time Marie's mother finished a story about how she had once accidentally pasted herself to a wall, the girl had drawn a picture and wanted to show it to me.

Other children love to be the center of attention in the session. They see the therapist as a new audience they can thrill with their knowledge of the world. Since parents and other family members are not impressed with information and performances they have heard and seen 1,000 times before, the child happily chats with the therapist, developing a trusting relationship in the process.

The younger the child, the more concrete is their thinking. For this reason, it is more effective to ask a young child specific, closed questions rather then abstract, open-ended ones. The therapist gains better information, for instance, by questioning the child about specific things the child's teacher does or does not do than by asking the child's opinion about school in general. Preschool children's thinking can also be highly syncretic, moving about on tangents, so casual conversation is often more productive than focused analysis.

A smart therapist stays current with childhood fads and trends. Nothing puts a child off worse than a reference to a dated topic. Of course, nonhip therapists can always admit their stupidity and encourage the child to enlighten them during a chat, as most children love to assume the role of expert.

Teenage Chatting

Adolescents are among the least willing participants in therapy. They are frequently brought into sessions by parents or agencies that are complaining about some behavior the teen doesn't see as a problem. Even in situations where the young persons are seeking help on their own initiative, they see the therapist as part of the authoritarian structure and/or as hopelessly outdated. Adolescent thinking is considerably more abstract than that of younger children, but this brings its own problems, as the teenager is painfully aware of what others think of them. This self-consciousness can result in a reluctance to speak because the adolescent worries about being judged by the therapist.

Rapport can often be established with teenagers by chatting about things that interest them in a noncritical manner. Their friends, school, fashion trends, rock groups, and personal hobbies can be useful topics of conversation and establish the therapist as someone who is approachable and capable of listening. When adolescents come for therapy with their families, they automatically assume that the therapist will side with other adults. If the therapist has not judged them during the chat, teens becomes more optimistic that their views will be heard.

> Juan, a 15-year-old Filipino boy, came for a session with his parents, two older brothers, and a little sister. His parents had not informed Juan why they were coming and two minutes into the appointment, when it became clear that the family was there to address Juan's substance abuse problem, he exploded. Juan was furious at being tricked, and he reacted by leaving the room, slamming the door, and knocking down several bulletin boards in

the hall. His mother said this was typical behavior for Juan. Whenever he was confronted, he went wild, which was why they had not told him the purpose of the visit prior to attending. The family was very quiet for the rest of the session.

Two weeks later, I received a phone call from Juan, asking if he could come to see me on his own. I agreed to meet with him without his family. Juan apologized for his behavior during the last session, but said he was furious at his mother for tricking him. Additionally, Juan was embarrassed at having his problems exposed in front of his siblings. I chatted with Juan about his drug use. We discussed the hottest drugs around town, how much they cost, and how to buy them. Juan explained the drug culture in detail and told me how being involved with drugs made him feel part of a group. After chatting about drugs for half of the session, Juan confided in me that he didn't use drugs as often as his parents thought, and he really wanted to stop because the issue was isolating him from his family. Juan also planned to be a veterinarian, and he knew that the drugs were messing up his grades. He agreed to have his family come to the next session, since he felt I would be fair in handling the situation.

Adult Chatting

Adults who come for therapy vary in how much they want to engage in chatting. Some adult clients are very problem focused and see irrelevant conversation as taking up unnecessary time. Others are so anxious about resolving their issues that they would rather chat than discuss sensitive topics. Adults are more socially adept than children, but they are also more bound by rules of interchange, and so are more willing to humor the therapist. Care should be taken to observe the effect the chatting is having on the client so that it is not imposed where it is not welcome.

Adults can chat on a wide range of issues, from politics to the weather. They often like to discuss issues regarding work or their children. Relaxed conversations about these topics can provide insight into relationships and situations relevant to the client's presenting and underlying problems. Adults willingly chat about hobbies, such as gardening or sports, and their reminiscences about previous interests often reveal dynamics related to their current issues. Chatting with the parents of a child who presents for treatment often uncovers hooks and tools that can be used to structure therapy.

John and Sally came to the session with their 15-year-old son, Brian. Brian was grossly overweight, unmotivated, and failing in school. We spent the first session discussing family history. Sally said she was concerned because John rarely spent time with his son, and Brian never listened to her because she was the only one talking. I suggested an intervention that the family might try during the following week. When they returned for the next session, we chatted briefly about the heavyweight championship bout scheduled for that evening. John said he had boxed in his youth, and had even made it to the Golden Gloves competition. He became excited in reminiscing about hitting the heavy punching bag and doing speed work as preparation for a big fight. I suggested that John might buy a similar bag so that he could help Brian improve his coordination and learn to protect himself from the boys who teased him. Brian liked the idea, so John agreed to find a bag. When the family returned two weeks later, the father and son told me they had joined a gym together and were working out every night. A follow-up a year later found Brian doing much better in school and training not only with his father, but with a professional boxer as well.

Instead of being viewed as a meaningless social interaction, chatting can be an important therapeutic tool. It is particularly useful in partial control situations where clients wish to give a therapist the power to help them, but cannot fully commit because they are afraid of change or of dealing with sensitive issues. Chatting can be effectively adjusted to meet the developmental level of any client. Therapists are best advised to find a relaxed style that is congruent with their own mode of functioning.

10

SUBSTITUTION

In many partial control situations, clients begin therapy anxious to resolve their problems. As therapy progresses, however, the client's ability to execute tasks decreases significantly. As much as clients wish to overcome their difficulties, they become powerless to do so. This could be a product of the client's personality, the context of the therapy, or the dynamics of the underlying problem. Whatever the cause, the client removes control from the therapist by withholding information or refusing to comply with suggestions.

Many therapists are stunned by the sudden withdrawal of cooperation by a client who had previously seemed motivated. They strive to develop "new and improved" interventions, certain that the right tool will bring the client back. The more ideas the therapist puts forward, however, the more such clients refuse, until they are unable to function in therapy at all.

As in other instances of partial control, the answer to the standoff is usually hidden in the underlying problem. In the method proposed in this chapter, the therapist shifts the focus from the client in order to hook them back into the therapeutic process. By effectively using family members, rather than the client, to address the client's issues, the struggle between the client and the therapist is eliminated. Clients are absolved from any responsibility in dealing with their presenting problems, which eventually enables them to remove the obstacles blocking the resolution of their issues.

The situation is analogous to that of parents who constantly try to get their teenagers to tidy their rooms. Despite requests, bribes, and threats, the room remains uncleaned. If, however, the parents decide to clean the room themselves, the teenager often springs into action to do the job.

METHOD

In the substitution technique, a family member or other relevant person takes over the responsibility of the presenting problem. In doing so, they remove any obligation by the client to work on the issue. This intervention should be used in situations in which clients have been unable to resolve their difficulties for themselves, despite a desire to overcome their problems. The following prerequisites must be met if the technique is to be effective.

1. The client and therapist must have tried unsuccessfully to resolve the presenting problem.

2. The client must feel powerless with regard to the problem or take a passive role in resolving it.

3. The client must be willing to allow another person to take over the attempt to resolve the problem.

4. The "substitute" must be cooperative with the therapist and willing to follow suggestions in order to resolve the client's problem.

5. The substitute must be linked to the underlying problem in some way.

PROCRASTINATION

Clients who appear in therapy for help with procrastination often have marginal success, since their problem, by definition, limits their ability to follow interventions in a timely fashion. Dick, age 26, entered my office looking uncertain and depressed. He was dressed well, but he continually toyed with an unkempt mustache. After an exchange of pleasantries, Dick detailed the issues that were bothering him. He stated that he was still living at home, attending the same state college where he began as a freshman seven years earlier. Every time Dick came close to completing a degree, he would change his major and start again. At this point, Dick had been in school so long that he was beginning to lose credits earned earlier. Currently, he was in the final semester of a business curriculum. He needed to make up three incompletes from the last semester and finish two courses in the present term in order to graduate. He said he wanted to attend interviews for postgraduation jobs, but he habitually arrived late for appointments, and usually without his resume. Dick felt unable to accomplish anything, adding that he even put off calling women he wanted to date.

Dick was adamant about keeping his family out of the sessions. He said he felt like a personal and financial drain on his parents, since they had already paid for three extra years of college and were footing the bill for the therapy. He was determined to show his father, a successful businessman, that he could resolve his difficulties on his own. His older brother was such a screw-up that Dick's parents spent most of their free time bailing him out. Dick wanted desperately to fix his problems himself.

I accepted Dick as an individual client on the condition that his family be included after one month if his problems did not change. While I felt that success was more likely in a family context, I realized that Dick would probably refuse therapy if I insisted on having his parents attend. We could attempt to address Dick's issues, and if they were resolved, his parents' participation would not be needed. If we were unsuccessful, the next step could be taken.

Dick and I developed an organizational plan to help him use his time more effectively. I tried to minimize his reluctance to enter the "real" world by discussing graduate school as a possibility. We examined issues that might be contributing to Dick's remaining an undergraduate and living at home, such as a wish to stay young, contemporary, or protected. Dick and I made lists of his positive accomplishments and established small, concrete goals. Despite our efforts and good intentions, however, he was no closer to resolving his procrastination one month into therapy than he had been at the beginning.

As previously agreed, Dick's parents accompanied him to the next session. I asked if I could meet with them privately, and Dick agreed. I explained to his parents that Dick had been trying very hard to overcome his procrastination but was unable to do so on his own. I asked if they would be willing to assist Dick by following my suggestions, and they readily acceded. I told them I felt Dick would be best helped by having his parents accomplish all of the tasks he had not completed. By doing so, they would model the appropriate way to finish projects and demonstrate their concern for him. Their actions would also serve as a benchmark for any difficulties Dick might encounter in the future.

I asked Dick back into the session and suggested that he write down for his parents the tasks he needed to accomplish to overcome his current problems. He listed eight items.

1. Finish all his incomplete courses from the last semester.

2. Do assignments and take exams in his current courses so he could pass this year.

3. Prepare a solid resume.

4. Buy and maintain an appropriate suit for interviews.

5. Attend three job interviews on time.

6. Keep his room and work materials organized.

7. Put aside money each week toward getting a place of his own.

8. Ask a certain woman for a date.

When Dick finished writing his list, I informed him that he needed to reduce his anxiety about accomplishing these tasks. He agreed with me, but stated that he didn't know how that could happen since he was so behind in his work. His parents proudly announced they would take care of the eight tasks to allow him time to become less stressed and more confident.

Dick was shocked and offered reasons why his parents wouldn't be able to accomplish the eight items. He knew his parents would be unable to pass his courses satisfactorily or finish his incompletes. He also felt that if his parents did assignments for him, he would be thrown out of school for turning in someone else's work. I suggested that Dick's parents might speak to his professors and explain their son's mental block in completing assignments. I added that even though his parents hadn't attended college for over 30 years and had no hope of maintaining Dick's "B" average, at least the work would be completed before he lost too many credits to graduate. His father added that he had just hired a young MBA, whom he could ask for assistance while completing Dick's work.

As horrified as Dick was by the thought that his parents would do his school assignments, he was totally distraught at the notion of his father's asking a woman out on a date for him. I reminded Dick that his father had managed to stay married for over 35 years and so must know how to treat women properly.

Dick continued to balk at the idea. He asked for two weeks in which to finish the eight tasks on his own. It was agreed that his parents would take over any uncompleted items at the end of that time. To everyone's amazement, including Dick's, he appeared for the session at the end of the two-week period with the tasks completed, except for one assignment which was being typed. One of his job interviews resulted in a job offer, contingent on his graduating. Dick was uncertain about accepting the position until his father asked whether he wanted him to send the young MBA to assist him in his new job.

A follow-up one year later found Dick living in an apartment with a friend, still employed, and dating several women. He told me that the primary motivation for his completing the tasks during therapy was not shame, but an appreciation of how much his parents cared for him. He realized that he didn't want to spend his life like his brother, always depending on his parents to succeed, but it was nice to know how much they cared.

DOLL HOUSE

Susan came to my office with her mother, father, and two dolls. She was a precocious seven-year-old, used to charming her way in and out of situations. Susan's parents, both school teachers, looked frazzled and tired. They were frustrated by Susan's continual lying and stealing. Every punishment possible had been attempted, from taking away TV privileges to washing her mouth out with soap. Susan didn't seem to mind any restriction. Even when threatened with "double" punishments, she wasn't dissuaded from lying or stealing. Her mother indicated that the girl almost relished the discipline more than the malicious acts themselves.

Susan had an older brother, Bill, nine years of age. Two years previously, the family had adopted a severely handicapped girl, Ann, who was now four years old. Ann was so brain damaged that she was unable to do much aside from lie on her mattress and babble sounds. Susan liked Ann and always spent time with her, stroking the girl and making her smile. The parents explained that Ann required so much care, that they couldn't spend as much time with their other children.

It seemed obvious, even a trite observation, that Susan was lying and stealing to get her parent's attention. I began by asking her mother and father to each spend 15 minutes a day concentrating on Susan. When the family returned the following week, Susan's parents reported being unable to comply with the suggestion. Her father said he was working at a second job after school and was too tired to interact with his daughter on a regular basis. Her mother also complained of being exhausted because Ann had suffered flu during the week. She added that Susan's lying and stealing made her so angry that even when she had the time she found it difficult to play with the girl since all she wanted to do was throttle her.

Susan interrupted to show me the three dolls she brought to the session, describing each in detail. The oldest was Elizabeth, eight and a half years old and a bad girl. Elizabeth hit the other dolls and spit on them. She never combed her hair and wore terrible clothes. If confronted about her behavior, Elizabeth would lie and talk back to her parents. Amanda was Elizabeth's sister and was six and a half. She picked up many bad habits from her sister. Jody, the youngest doll, was always good. She kissed a lot and would hug everyone to make them feel better. Jody sang herself to sleep, and everyone loved her. Susan mentioned there were three other dolls at home, each with a distinctive personality.

I asked Susan's father if he would mind taking the girl for a walk. Once we were alone, I commiserated with Susan's mother about how difficult it was to manage a job, a handicapped child, and a daughter with defiant behavior. I suggested she needed a vacation from dealing with Susan. In place of disciplining the girl, which was having little effect, or spending time with her, which proved unpalatable, I suggested that Susan's mother spend 15 minutes an evening playing with Susan's dolls. She could punish them as needed and nurture them as required. This would model acceptable behavior for Susan, and also let the girl know what actions pleased and displeased her mother. Susan's mother could even let the girl help her punish the dolls or give them love. Despite thinking I was crazy, her mother agreed to the plan.

When the family returned two weeks later, there was a big change in their demeanor. Susan and her mother were able to joke with each other, and her father looked less harried. The parents had easily followed the plan and actually took turns playing with the dolls. Susan enjoyed this contact with her parents, and everyone appreciated the rest from dealing with Susan's misbehavior. The girl's lying and stealing diminished significantly over the two-week period, with no episodes during the past three days.

By substituting the dolls for Susan as the focus of the mother's anger, I was able to address Susan's underlying problem. She could receive love and attention from her parents in a form acceptable to them. The impasse preventing the resolution of the presenting problem was successfully circumvented.

A six-month follow-up with the family revealed no recurrence of the stealing or lying. The parents' current concern was Susan's academic performance, so we discussed some ways to give her extra help. As an aside, her mother mentioned that Susan continued to have dolls in her bedroom, but rarely played with them, as she now preferred soccer and horseback riding. Her father was the coach of the soccer team, and the two of them enjoyed sharing the activity.

GRANDMOTHER BECOMES FATHER

The Byrd family came to the initial therapy session expectant, but uncertain. Mrs. Byrd worked as a loan officer at a local bank. Mr. Byrd had taken over his father's auto repair shop when he died eight years earlier, and his mother kept the books for him, as she had for her husband. The couple was a study in contrasts. Mrs. Byrd prided herself on her stylish clothes and high level of grooming, Mr. Byrd was unkempt and irritable. Whereas Mrs. Byrd maintained a cheerful, articulate interaction, Mr. Byrd grunted short replies. Their two sons were almost mirrors of the parents' presentation. Bill, age 18, dressed sharply, like his mother, and Ken, age 20, was a younger version of his father. The family wanted therapy because the two young men were having problems with intoxicants. Bill worked busing tables in an expensive restaurant, which gave him access to a variety of drugs. He was a refined user, with cocaine his drug of choice. Ken binged on alcohol, which usually resulted in his being laid off from his jobs. At the time of the first appointment, Ken had been accepted into a diesel mechanic training school and wanted to stay sober enough to enter the program.

Both sons had difficulties with their parents. Bill's interactions with his father were highly antagonistic, and his relationship with his mother was intense and explosive. His drug use had aged him beyond his 18 years, and he was jumpy and anxious during the session. Ken presented as more depressed. His father alternated between defending Ken's drinking and threatening to throw him out of the house. Mr. Byrd said he did not see a problem with alcohol—he used it extensively himself— he just couldn't understand why Ken let it mess up his life. Mrs. Byrd berated her husband and defended her sons, saying all of their problems were caused by their father's refusal to spend time with them and his constant drinking.

Initial therapy strategies centered on having the father take a more active role in the family. Mr. Byrd was asked to model for Ken the appropriate way of using alcohol, and the parents were encouraged to present a united front with regard to Bill's drug use. After three months, Bill stopped all drugs except marijuana. Ken was unable to limit his drinking and was apprehensive about entering the diesel training program. He had lost another job, and Mr. Byrd derided him as a stupid bum who couldn't make a living. Mrs. Byrd despaired of her sons ever being successes as long as her husband continued to drink.

The one person of whom everyone in the family spoke well was the paternal grandmother. While Mrs. Byrd resented the way her mother-in-law managed the family business and felt the woman often dismissed her as silly, she also respected her as a strong, capable woman. I asked if I could invite her to the next session, and the family agreed.

The older Mrs. Byrd presented as a take-charge woman in control of her family. I hypothesized to the group that a large part of the family's problems were caused by the parents' disagreements about the father's drinking. This caused stress and didn't allow them to work together. I suggested that the grandmother might take over as head of the household. Since Mr. Byrd worked long hours, his mother would be more available to the family than he could ever be. Because the father wouldn't be in charge of the family, his wife could stop pestering him about his drinking. He could do whatever he wanted with his time and let his family problems be solved by the two strong women. Mr. Byrd protested at first, questioning whether a woman his mother's age should be saddled with this responsibility. I commented that everyone younger had tried to solve the problem, with no success. Perhaps an older, more mature approach was needed.

The two women and I crafted a plan to resolve the family's issues. We decided that the primary goals should center on finding and keeping employment for Ken and getting Bill completely clean of drugs. The two women conferred on a daily basis. They established a "no criticism" rule within the family, which included Mrs. Byrd's view of her husband's drinking. Mr. Byrd was free to drink alcohol or abstain. The women asked him to concentrate on becoming a better friend to his sons, giving them moral support, but not worrying about enforcing any rules.

Within the month, Bill had stopped his drug use, and Ken was sober and employed. I suggested that the two women should be compensated for their hard work and success. Mr. Byrd could drive them to the restaurant where Bill worked, and pick them up after a nice meal. The women were ecstatic over the idea, and everyone looked forward to the event, except Mr. Byrd.

After another month, Ken had lost interest in his new job and threatened to quit. The grandmother complained she was exhausted, that this was her son's responsibility to fix. Mr. Byrd, largely ignored and subservient during the past few months, forced both women to plead with him before he agreed to reestablish his position in the household. Once they capitulated, he announced he had decided to quit drinking in order to act as a more successful model for his son.

In this case, control was withheld from the therapist because the father resented his wife's reaction to his drinking. By substituting his own mother in his position within the family, the father lost his power. When his status was reinstated at a later time, he was able to use his elevation in position to take the steps necessary for successful resolution of his sons' problems. Another key element to the success of this intervention was that by the grandmother's conferring status on her daughter-in-law, the way was paved for the husband and wife to work together.

BE MY WIFE, PLEASE!

Eddie, age 47, came for therapy because of marriage problems. Eddie had recently married for the fourth time, but things weren't working out well. Angela and Eddie had lived together for two years prior to getting married. At the wedding, Angela's mother deeded the house across the street from her own to the newlyweds. The couple terminated the lease on Eddie's apartment and moved into their new home. Eddie was horrified when he first saw the place. It was loaded with boxes from Angela's mother's house, each filled with mementos of Angela's life. Eddie began to realize that neither Angela nor her mother ever threw anything out. Every scrap from the past, from Angela's first baby tooth to her last husband's gardening clothes, had been saved. There were so many boxes that Eddie could barely walk through a room.

To make matters worse, much of the house was in disrepair. Angela refused to spend money to fix the plumbing or electrical wiring, insisting that it would be a slight to her mother to have repair persons come to the house. When Eddie knocked over some potted plants that were stored in the tub, blocking the drain with dirt and rendering the shower unusable, he concluded enough was enough.

Because this was his fourth marriage, Eddie was nervous about its failing. He decided to conceal the problems by going to live with his parents during the week. Eddie's mother was always protective of him, and he knew he could count on her to help him out. His main problem with his mother centered on his eating, as she criticized Eddie for being too thin and wouldn't stop pushing food at him. Eddie's relationship with his father, an eminent doctor with a string of personal and athletic successes to his name, had always been rocky. Being poor at science and physically frail, Eddie felt he was a disappointment to the older man. Despite having several advanced degrees, Eddie often needed his father to bail him out financially, as he never seemed to hold a job very long. He had been unemployed for four years before starting a consultant business. Because Eddie usually worked as a part-time employee, he had no benefits, and his income was tenuous.

Eddie would return to Angela on weekends. They enjoyed each other's company and continued their positive sexual relationship. On Sundays, he would go back to his parents' house and stay with them until the following Friday night. Eddie was happy with the arrangement, but Angela and his parents seemed to be getting annoyed. His parents were pushing him either to fix his home life or to get a divorce and move into a place of his own. Angela resented his parents and felt they were turning Eddie against her.

My first attempts at therapy centered on Eddie's relationship with his wife and his reluctance to confront her about the house. Although he appeared eager to improve his relationship with Angela, he never carried out suggestions, always coming up with an excuse for why he couldn't attempt them. It became apparent that Eddie was in a comfortable situation in which he was finally getting positive attention from his parents, especially his father. It became clear that the problem would not be resolved in its current state.

Eddie agreed to bring his parents to the next session. His father and mother were well groomed and articulate. They clearly loved their son and were anxious to help him, but it was also obvious that they wanted him out of their house. Mrs. Sabatini had recently retired from a supervisory position and looked forward to a life without children or job responsibilities. She prided herself on a meticulous, orderly home, and Eddie had never been tidy. She was ashamed to have neighbors drop by, afraid what they would say about the appearance of her house or the state of her son's marriage. Dr. Sabatini was furious that his daughter-in-law was neglecting his son. He alternated between goading Eddie into being a man and commiserating with his plight. Both parents were afraid that Eddie would lose his job once again if he did not have clean clothes to wear or a comfortable place in which to live.

I asked the family to make a list of the things they felt Angela should do for Eddie as his wife. They came up with five items.

1. Share a home with Eddie and be his companion.

2. Keep a clean, tidy home.

3. Provide nutritious meals for Eddie so he wouldn't be so thin.

4. Assist Eddie with his work.

5. Make sure that Eddie had clean clothes for work.

I suggested that as Dr. and Mrs. Sabatini were much more capable of filling the requirements than was Angela, perhaps they should take over as Eddie's "wife." Mrs. Sabatini always kept a clean house and made good meals for her son. She did a good job with Eddie's laundry and made sure that he was presentable for work. Dr. Sabatini was bright and articulate and could be not only a good companion, but a positive role model for Eddie. He could help him with strategies for keeping his jobs and also give him advice on extending his consultancy contracts. I reminded the parents how worried they were that Eddie would fail once again, and how much better he was doing since he had returned home. I asked the family to imagine how far Eddie could go if they devoted another two years of care to him.

The family seemed shocked. No one felt that the current situation should continue for two more years. Mrs. Sabatini insisted that a man was better off with his wife than with his parents. I reminded her that she and her husband would be much more capable than Angela of fulfilling the duties on the list. Eddie wasn't sure he wanted to commit to being with his parents for two years. Dr. Sabatini wavered between defending Eddie and protecting his wife. I asked the family to consider my idea, stating that two additional years of caring for their son was a small price to pay for his success.

Four days later, I received a phone call from Eddie. His parents had located a small apartment for him, with a cleaning service and a laundry close by. They felt he'd be better off there during the week and were willing to finance the rental. In thinking about the move, Eddie realized that he'd rather be with his wife than alone in an apartment. He told Angela he'd rather live with her than without her, and asked her help in making the marriage work. Angela agreed to rent a storage unit for the boxes and arranged to have a plumber come while her mother was on vacation.

Substitution can be a powerful technique for clients yielding partial control. By enlisting the help of a family member, the client no longer has to struggle with resolving the presenting problem. If the substitution is linked to the client's underlying issues, the technique has enough power to help the client break free of the factors limiting success and regain control of the presenting problems.

11

THE IMPERFECT CLIENT

Most therapists enter practice with visions of perfect clients dancing in their head. A parade of cooperative clients with resolvable problems present for treatment, anxious to have the therapist employ an array of brilliant, creative interventions to improve their lives and illuminate their issues. The therapist has only to offer the barest of suggestions or a glimmer of insight before the clients spring into appropriate action, thus gaining constructive resolution of all of their problems. The clients thank the therapist for his or her inspiration and help before heading out of the office into the sunset.

Life doesn't always imitate artful imaginings. Many clients who walk through the door bear little resemblance to the ideal client. To the dismay of many therapists whose theoretical orientations are based on cooperation, the client doesn't always play by the rules. In no case is this more apparent or frustrating than in a client who is a master of the illusion of control, the Imperfect Client.

Imperfect Clients appear in the office, desperate for relief from their problems. Unfortunately, they have difficulty explaining to the therapist exactly what their issues are or who is involved in them. Their abstractions and vagaries are difficult to pin down by either gentle or pointed questioning. These clients know they are suffering, but they are either unable or unwilling to define why. As the therapist struggles for a handle on the issues, the client evades any explanation but escalates the complaints. With the client begging for help, the therapist introduces suggestion after suggestion, each of which the client deems inappropriate or impossible to carry out. Any call for action is met with inertia. Imperfect Clients are experts at watching frustrated therapists work harder to resolve their problems than they do. The Herculean efforts by the therapist, however, are rarely appreciated and frequently criticized.

There are a number of reasons why Imperfect Clients might present this illusion of control to a therapist. Some of them have personality issues that prevent them from yielding control to a therapist even though they are in need of help. Others have a history of ineffectual therapy that makes them wary and pessimistic about positive outcomes. Some Imperfect Clients are apprehensive about solving their problems because of the changes this would make in their lives. Many Imperfect Clients have developed a "learned helplessness" reaction to their problems. Their difficulties have been so severe, so chronic, or so immutable, that they see themselves as powerless to effect a change. The ownership of their problem is often the only vestige of control they have left. Whatever the reason, all Imperfect Clients have difficulty relinquishing control despite wanting the therapist's assistance.

This control issue permeates all levels of the therapeutic interaction. Imperfect Clients have difficulty complying with the simplest aspects of therapy. They often do not show up for appointments, pay their fees, or bring in relevant family members. Imperfect Clients complain when a therapist terminates their session to see another client, even if the session was short because they arrived 40 minutes late.

Since therapists often become frustrated in these situations, they tend to minimize the client's complaints and deny their suffering. Imperfect Clients are dismissed as resistant, manipulative, and difficult. In reality, these clients often have quite severe problems, complicated by their extreme control issues. Imperfect Clients withhold control from the therapist, but they also desperately want the therapist to help them. To be effective, therapy would have to utilize this difficult position to resolve the client's issues.

METHOD

It is easy to identify Imperfect Clients by observing their behavior during the early phases of therapy. The following characteristics are often present.

1. The client is frequently late for therapy appointments, if they have not canceled at the last minute or not shown at all.

2. When questioned about why they did not appear for a session, Imperfect Clients usually blame their emotions. They do not like to come to therapy when feeling happy, as the session might jeopardize their good mood. They also cannot get motivated to come when depressed.

3. When asked to describe their problem, Imperfect Clients use vague, abstract terms, such as overwhelmed, depressed, or anxious. Some Imperfect Clients are at a loss to connect these feelings to any events or people in their lives. Others can describe the difficult situations of their lives in graphic detail, but see themselves as powerless in relation to their problems.

4. Goals are equally vague or perceived as unattainable. Imperfect Clients may wish to be "happy" or "less stressed," but do not see attainment of that state as possible. Additionally, these clients have no idea how they would know if they reached their goal because concrete definitions prove elusive.

5. Imperfect Clients refuse to bring in relevant family members or partners. They assert that their problems belong only to them. No other person has been suffering as they have, and no one else is capable of helping them resolve these personal issues.

6. The appointment is punctuated with cries for help or statements about how depressed or anxious they are.

7. Imperfect Clients at some point will allude to their real issues, indicating that there is a secret they are not letting the therapist know. This gives the therapist the impression that, with enough understanding, intelligence, or persistence, the therapist will be able to uncover the client's core problem and address it effectively.

8. The therapy session often finds the therapist working harder than the client to resolve the client's issues. Imperfect Clients

dismiss the therapist's suggestions as too difficult, too time consuming, too confusing, or as having been previously attempted without success. They combine this criticism with renewed expressions of despair, prompting the therapist to come up with another round of interventions, which are also refused.

9. At the end of the hour, Imperfect Clients profess having problems finding the time for another session. They also experience difficulty with paying for the therapy.

10. These clients have often tried therapy a number of times before, but attribute the failure of treatment to the severity of their issues or to a problem with the therapist.

While not all Imperfect Clients show all of these characteristics, they usually demonstrate a significant number of them. In every case, however, Imperfect Clients combine their request for help with an inability to comply with suggestions.

Traditional therapy fails miserably with these clients. There are, however, two approaches that often are successful with Imperfect Clients because they prevent the therapist from engaging in control struggles. In the first technique, the therapist confronts such clients with their "imperfect" behavior, describing their typical style of responding in an effort to make them accountable for their actions. This technique usually is not effective in terminating the behavior because the clients' problems are often embedded in their control issues. It does, however, explain to the clients their responsibility in the therapeutic relationship. This technique should always be tried first, but if it does not produce adequate results, the second solution should be attempted.

In the second approach, the therapist turns control of the therapy completely over to the client. Because the Imperfect Clients' control issues supersede their ability to resolve their other problems, the therapist must also stop trying to resolve either the client's presenting problem or underlying issues. By yielding to them, the therapist enables Imperfect Clients to use their control eventually to resolve their own difficulties.

In this technique, the following instructions are given to the client.

1. No appointments are to be scheduled. Clients call on the day they want to see the therapist. Every effort will be made to accommodate them on that day.

2. Clients will come alone to the session or bring whomever they feel will be helpful.

3. The only suggestion ever given during therapy will be for the clients to pay attention to their symptoms in order to understand them better. They may attend to the duration, intensity, or location of their symptoms. They may record what happens before or during the problem or may watch the reactions of others.

4. Therapy sessions will be a forum where the clients present what they have learned about their problems. No insight or direction will be given by the therapist.

5. The goal of the therapy is for the clients to "feel better."

6. The clients will pay whatever they think is appropriate for the session.

The method is designed to assist Imperfect Clients by utilizing their need for control in an active manner, rather than their typical pattern of controlling others by passive, ambiguous behavior. As therapists restrain themselves from taking responsibility for the therapy, clients are able to use their own resources to change either their control issues or their presenting problems. Clients' commitment to change is enhanced by their active participation and by being the source of the solution. Typically, after several sessions in which the therapist adheres to this position, the clients reveal their "secret" issues and ask to address them. Therapists should be cautious and resist the temptation to regain control of the sessions too quickly. If authority is seized by the therapist precipitously, the Imperfect Client often reverts to a passive, helpless role.

KIM

Kim was 15 minutes late for her first session. She rushed into the office and threw herself into a chair. Although Kim was an attractive, well-educated 25-year-old, she said she felt her life was a mess. After graduating from college with a bachelor's degree, the only job she could land was as a waitress. To make matters worse, her lack of income necessitated that she move in with her brother and sister-in-law. Apart from a high level of groaning, Kim was extremely vague about exactly what was upsetting her. She would get teary every time I mentioned her past or her family, but except for throwing me a look that suggested there was something too sensitive to discuss, Kim always changed the subject back to the misery of her current situation. She said she hated living with her brother, and that she wanted a better job, but she doubted therapy could help her. There had been six previous therapists in the past, all of whom had been unsuccessful at resolving her problems. She did think that one of the therapists might have been helpful, if she hadn't terminated with him after he made a pass at her.

I discussed with Kim the possibility of having significant people in her life come to therapy to help with her problems. Kim dismissed the idea outright. Her parents had died years before, and she didn't want her brother attending, since he was part of the problem. When I suggested that might be the best reason to have him attend, Kim said there was no point to his coming, since she was too overwhelmed to work on her problems anyway. I gave Kim several ideas to think about over the next week. She said she didn't know if she'd have time to try them, since waitressing kept her fairly busy. Kim then pleaded for a discount on the fee, as she was trying to save all her money to get out of her current mess.

Kim canceled her next appointment a week later but managed to show on time the following week. She hadn't tried any of my suggestions because her problems were sapping all of her energy. I mentioned a few other ideas to her that might require less stamina, but Kim dismissed them, saying she had already worked on similar things with her previous therapists. Kim started to cry, sobbing that she couldn't understand why I didn't see how miserable she was and help her.

I didn't have much hope of ameliorating any of Kim's problems in the current context. I suggested to her that perhaps the reason I couldn't help her was because she wouldn't let me try. No matter what I proposed, Kim rejected or refused the idea. I asked her if she realized that she kept obstructing the therapy by not letting me participate.

Kim denied she was controlling any part of the process. She maintained that all she wanted was a decent job so she could get her own place, one where she'd feel comfortable bringing a friend. She said she didn't know why this was too difficult for me to solve. I decided that Kim would benefit from the Imperfect Client technique, that this might be the only way to invest her in therapy. I sympathized with the degree of suffering Kim was experiencing and suggested we structure our sessions to entail the least amount of discomfort. Kim was to call only on the days she wanted to see me, she would pay only the amount she could afford, and I would stop putting forward ideas that caused her stress. Between the sessions, Kim was to focus on her problem. Using the excellent skills she had acquired during her college days, Kim could collect information relevant to her situation. She might write down what was happening when she felt bad or when she felt good, and use her trained mind to analyze the situation. Perhaps once she learned more about her problems, I could be successful in helping her.

Kim called twice for appointments during the next month, and I fit her into my schedule at the next available time. Kim said she'd been doing a lot of thinking, and that she realized that all of her problems seemed linked to a feeling she was like a doormat. Her parents had always imposed on her, and now she put herself into situations where others could also treat her badly. I resisted the temptation to offer either tasks or insights to Kim and suggested she continue her progress and good work.

I didn't hear from Kim again. Several months later, I received a call from her brother, requesting marriage counseling. Kim had suggested he see me because her therapy had been so successful. She was now living in a major city, working in a responsible job for a well-known magazine, with an apartment and a live-in boyfriend. It seemed that by my yielding during therapy with Kim, instead of struggling with her control issues, I enabled her to resolve her problems.

DEBORAH

Deborah was 30 years old, and she was depressed. She moaned that no one should have to go through the life she had endured so far. Her mother was a "mental case" who committed suicide three years previously. Deborah's father walked out when Deborah was 10 and never looked back. He remarried soon after his departure and had never shown any interest in her at all. Deborah learned at an early age to look after herself, but it seemed as though she was always in a mess. She married Jim when she turned 20. He abused her physically throughout their marriage, and still called her even though they had separated five years earlier. She was currently in a relationship with Ken, who treated her very well. Deborah has a five-year-old daughter and worked part-time as a legal secretary.

I asked Deborah what she wanted out of therapy. She said she was always depressed and just wanted to feel better. She didn't want anyone else to accompany her to the therapy sessions, because she wanted the time all to herself. After listening to her history and offering some suggestions, a second appointment was scheduled for a week later.

Deborah called on the morning of her session to say she was feeling really good that day and didn't want to ruin it by coming in for therapy. Another appointment was scheduled, and also canceled, this time because Deborah was feeling too depressed to come in. I suggested that Deborah should call for her next appointment only when she felt the mood was just right.

A few days later, Deborah rang me in an agitated state. Ken drove her to the session, but she insisted he wait in the car. I asked Deborah what was upsetting her, and she repeated all of the details from the first session. She added that she didn't know why she had come to see me, since nobody could fix such a miserable life.

I commiserated with Deborah and said that the first step toward feeling better would be to gain control over the therapy sessions. She was in no shape to tackle her whole life, but maybe she would feel better if she was at least able to decide what happened between us. Deborah was to call when her mood was right, set her own fees, and discuss only things she wanted. She agreed to the plan, and during the next two sessions, she focused on different ways she could take charge of her life.

For the fourth session, Deborah asked to include her boyfriend, Ken. They explained that Deborah's estranged husband, Jim, was becoming a real nuisance. He called all the time and disrupted the entire household. Deborah wanted to file for divorce but was afraid of how Jim might respond. Ken spent much of the session reassuring her by describing how he would protect her. We discussed various ways of handling Jim's intrusions, and the couple left.

Two more sessions were held with both Ken and Deborah. Divorce proceedings were initiated, and even when Jim became upset and threatened her, Deborah remained firm in her decision. She asked me to contact her lawyer, and I agreed to provide assistance. I didn't hear from Deborah until two years after her divorce. She and Ken were now having some difficulties in their relationship, and they wanted help in ironing them out. Deborah laughingly assured me that they would show up for their appointment, if I gave them one for the following week.

MARY

When Mary called on the phone, she stated she had just recovered from a two-week bout of depression. She said that she longed to be a happier person and to gain better insight into her problems. Mary worked as a social worker and indicated that a colleague had suggested that she suffered from "agitated depression." Mary added that she could be quite good at fooling people about how badly she felt, and that even her husband, despite their warm and loving relationship, didn't know she was unhappy, much less depressed.

Mary canceled her first appointment and came at the wrong time for her second session. She insisted that I had written down the incorrect time and day and was very upset at having to come back. We finally made it to the same appointment on the third try. Mary was 27 years old, but looked considerably older, and her first comments during the session concerned her feeling tired. She said she couldn't believe how fatigued she became from just going to work and taking care of her husband and two children. Her mother had been sick most of her life, having contracted tuberculosis as a teenager, and heart problems and lupus as an adult. Despite all of this, and caring for six children, Mary never remembered hearing her mother complain of being tired. Mary said she wished she had her mother's strong mind and determination. She despaired that she was more like her father, a perfectionist who became angry whenever things didn't go his way. Despite these similarities to her father, Mary's mother was the only one in the family to whom she felt close.

Mary started crying and said she lacked control over her life. Because of her mother's illnesses, Mary worried constantly about her own health and that of her husband and children. She was afraid of having panic attacks, even though she had never experienced one, and thought constantly of death.

I sympathized with Mary and agreed that she had a lot of worries with which to contend. I asked her if there were a particular issue on which she would like to start working. Mary moaned that there were so many it was difficult to choose only one. I suggested that she make a list of all of her problems in the order in which we should address them. Mary said that would be impossible since she had difficulty setting priorities. I suggested she could include that on her list.

Mary began the next session by complaining about being there. She was so tired, she couldn't believe that she had added another commitment to her life. Mary said she couldn't really afford therapy, especially when she was too overwhelmed to work on any of her problems. Her last attempt at therapy had failed as well, since her therapist had moved to another state before solving Mary's problems.

The Imperfect Client strategy seemed appropriate for Mary's case, as she was resistant to any direct suggestions. I described the procedure to her, and after some initial hesitation, she agreed to try it. She contacted me two weeks later and asked for an appointment. In the time between sessions, Mary had decided to keep a diary of her feelings. She presented me with eight pages of notebook paper describing her emotions over the past two weeks. Mary stated that the act of writing down and then analyzing things forced her to evaluate her goals in life. When she looked at the context for most of her bad feelings, she realized they originated in her own head. Mary was determined to develop some of her mother's courage to resolve them.

Mary requested five more sessions during the next three months. Therapy during the first three consisted of her presenting her diary and commenting on her feelings. She noted how her depression was beginning to improve, and I encouraged her to keep track of every aspect of her development. By the fourth session, Mary was soliciting some advice on particular issues. I gave her some suggestions for resolving the problems, but made it clear that she didn't need to follow my recommendations since she had done so well on her own. By the fifth session, Mary said she felt comfortable in terminating therapy.

I received a postcard from her about a year later. Since our last session, Mary said, her mother had almost died and two of her friends were in serious car accidents. Despite the pressure, Mary avoided sinking into depression by focusing on the good things in her family and work.

In the preceding cases, it was demonstrated how yielding to an Imperfect Client's illusion of control can produce success rather than frustration in therapy. Instead of the therapists striving for an ever better direct intervention, they can turn therapy over to the clients, allowing them to use their need for control to resolve their presenting and underlying problems. It is important that therapists allow the clients to take credit for this success. Failure to do so would result in the clients' doubting their ability to handle their own problems, leading to a recurrence of their issues. While the Imperfect Client technique might be awkward or difficult for some therapists, it is still less frustrating than trying to analyze problems a client never fully describes or presenting brilliant interventions that are never tried.

12

"LET'S MAKE A DEAL"

One of the most difficult groups of illusion of control clients are those who present for therapy with a sense of hopelessness and despair. They have been repeatedly unsuccessful in solving their problems and have developed the pattern of learned helplessness. The clients keep the therapist involved with their problems by acting desperate and asking for help. Any suggestions by the therapist, however, are met with inaction by the client, punctuated by claims that their problems are too insurmountable for things to improve. Despite their pleas for assistance and support, the clients seem more interested in talking about their problems than in changing them. The clients use the therapist as a sounding board for all of the reasons they cannot take action, but are not generally receptive when the therapist suggests solutions.

Clients with these levels of hopeless feelings usually portray themselves as victims of someone else's actions. This is often evident in the case of parents who feel they are suffering because of their children's behavior. These parents often say that they feel like hostages in their own homes and have a sense of being emotionally blackmailed by their own child. They believe their predicament will only be resolved by an improvement in their child and deemphasize their own role in the situation.

> John, age 10, refused to attend school. When his parents
> insisted that he go, he would become violent and destroy
> things in the home. The more his parents pressured John,
> the more destructive he would become. His parents said
> they were overwhelmed by the severity of John's behavior,
> which had gone on for two years. While they actively
> sought my advice during therapy, they always rejected any
> suggestions, claiming that any action on their part would

lead to an increase in John's violent behavior. Despite their reluctance to alter their own behavior, they would telephone me daily to complain about John.

Another group of clients who regularly show this helpless form of illusion of control are adults who feel trapped and overwhelmed by a spouse's behavior. In these circumstances, the clients focus on the conduct of their spouses and fear to take action on their own. If a therapist pushes these clients to take control of their own lives, they usually resist, claiming that no action on their part can fix the problem, since it belongs to their spouse.

Barbara, age 43, sought therapy because of her husband's eight-year drinking problem. She had been married to Carl for the past 17 years. Barbara claimed to be unhappy in her life and blamed it on Carl's drinking. Although she led an independent life, she craved a romantic, intimate relationship with a partner. Barbara cried often during the session. She was depressed about growing older and expressed a desire to get out of her present situation with Carl before it was too late to matter. When I offered several suggestions, Barbara sobbed and said it was useless to take any action, because the problem was caused by Carl's drinking and not her own behavior. Besides, she said, she was afraid that if she upset Carl, she would end up alone.

The pattern of illusion of control attributable to feelings of helplessness can also be seen in adult clients who are unable to resolve their problems because of their relationship with their parents. The clients often present as desperate for help, but resist change because of their parents' perceived influence on them.

Jesse came to his first therapy session enormously overweight and unemployed, despite two professional degrees. He said he needed help to improve his self-esteem so he could find a job that paid good money. Jesse reported difficulty in getting along with both his tyrannical father, who failed to appreciate him, and his mother, who treated him like a child. I offered Jesse several suggestions for working on the problems he presented. He responded that he was too upset over his parents' treatment to work on solving any of his problems. He added, however, that he desperately wanted my help as his life was too depressing in its current state.

METHOD

The following technique was developed as a solution for working successfully with clients who present an illusion of control due to feeling helpless and/or hopeless. It was designed to produce a rapid effect and place power in the hands of those who professed impotence. The method was developed from a popular game show in the 1970s called "Let's Make a Deal," in which a contestant would choose one of three doors, knowing that behind one of the doors was a booby prize. Part of the suspense of the game was based on the contestants' not knowing what prize they would be getting. In this therapeutic approach, the client is analogously given an active role in selecting an approach without knowing for sure what the result will be. The use of the Let's Make a Deal format often adds humor to a situation in which clients have felt powerless about making decisions.

The technique will be described and illustrated using cases involving young adults who would not leave home. In an ideal world, persons entering young adulthood have mastered the skills needed for independent living. They are excited about disengaging from parental control and eager to continue their development without having their basic needs met by their parents. In the best-case scenario, the parents are also delighted that their child is leaving home and look forward to having more time for raising their other children or enjoying life on their own.

Unfortunately, this scenario does not always play out as planned. Young adults may not have developed sufficient maturity to cope with independent living, or they do not possess the financial or psychological resources for doing so. When their parents pressure them to leave, they engage in provocative behavior toward the family or develop a symptom, such as depression or drug addiction, that makes it difficult for the family to expect them to leave.

In other cases, the young adults, or the conflict about their staying in the home, may be serving some dynamic within the family. Their presence may be necessary to buffer marital disagreements. Conversely, fights over the young adult's remaining in the home may keep parents from focusing on other family issues, such as alcoholism or infidelity.

Families entering therapy in these situations often present as frustrated, helpless parents dragging in an uncooperative young adult. Often the parents are too defeated to listen to the therapist's suggestions and are divided on what constitutes an acceptable solution. The young adult is usually uncooperative, if he or she attends the sessions at all. The entire family wants an instant resolution to their problem, as they have lost the patience to undergo extensive therapy. Their cooperation is usually tenuous, however, and they frequently do not follow the therapist's suggestions.

In the Let's Make a Deal technique, the therapist asks the entire family to attend the first session. If the young adult fails to attend the first or any subsequent session, or if the young adult attends but is clearly uncooperative, the therapist works with the parents and other family members who show up. The young adult is generally isolated from the process, although the therapist may choose to see them individually to address problems they are having independent of the family. As a result, the young adult may remain involved in the therapeutic process but is kept powerless in the family decision making. This is critical, because young adults often hold the balance of control in the family because of their behavior.

During the first session, the therapist gathers information from the family, paying special attention to their previous, failed attempts at solving the problem. At the completion of the first session, the therapist tells the family, without the young adult present, that, to the best of the therapist's knowledge, there are only three solutions to this problem. Two of the solutions could lead to a resolution of their difficulty. The therapist presents the three solutions as "doors," as in "Let's Make a Deal." The three choices are as follows:

Door 1—An authoritative approach whereby the parents target specific behaviors and demand compliance from the young adult on those issues.

The therapist instructs the family that strength and benevolent power are crucial ingredients of this choice. By modeling the appropriate use of power, the parents will teach their child how to obtain control over his or her own life. The therapist tells the parents initially to select three rules and consequences. Siblings and other family members are to assist the parents in implementing the plan. Families should contact the therapist if they weaken in their resolve between appointments, especially since young adults usually escalate their behavior in response to control. It is essential that the family present as a united front and that all members agree with the stated rules and consequences.

Door 2—A maintenance approach whereby the family is encouraged to keep behaving exactly as they have in the past.

This door is usually chosen by clients who are not ready to change their behavior at this phase of therapy. After obtaining a detailed account of all of the ways the parents have previously tried to resolve their child's problem and failed, the therapist summarizes for the family how their behavior patterns keep them in a homeostatic sequence. The therapist explains the role of each family member in the situation and how that member perpetuates the pattern through his or her actions. The therapist assures the family that, if they continue in this manner, nothing will change. The benefit of choosing door 2 lies in the comfort and predictability of their behavior. Therapy can be used as a forum to express their frustration over the continuance of the problem and receive empathy from the therapist.

Door 3—An unconditional-love approach where the parents accept all of the young adult's behavior without criticism.

The therapist instructs the parents to love the young adult unconditionally, being highly empathetic and genuine. In this way, their child's pathological behavior resolves as the child loses his or her feelings of being neglected and misunderstood. The parents should express their care throughout the day and protect the young adult from any undue stress or discomfort. The parents are to place no pressure on their child and only show tolerance and compassion in their actions. If struggles develop, the parents are to exaggerate their caring so that their child will fully appreciate their concern.

After describing the three doors, the therapist asks the family to choose the one that fits their style and resources the best. The family is asked to discuss the merits of each choice and agree on the door they select. The therapist accepts whatever choice the family makes and thus does not fight the family for control of the process. By yielding to their decision, the therapist places control within the family itself, short-circuiting the struggle that is the hallmark of illusion of control. The Let's Make a Deal approach provides the therapist with a tool for resolving the family's control issues within the context of their presenting problem.

The strength of the technique lies in the three concrete alternatives presented to the family. Because the choices are finite, and because the therapist asserts they are the only three choices of which the therapist is aware, the family must either select one of the doors or resolve the problem on their own.

The need to make a choice often creates a stir in the family. Often the family will counter with the idea that they would rather kick their child out of the house or put the child into the hospital. The therapist should comment that getting rid of their child in this manner doesn't resolve the problem but only delays their choice, since their child will inevitably return to their home. If the family feels a need to delay their decision while seeking hospitalization, the therapist can recess therapy until the family decides to resume outpatient treatment.

If the family is unable to reach a decision during the therapy session about which door to select, they are instructed to return the following week with a unanimous decision. It is the agreement to take a unified position that increases the success of the intervention. At times, it may be necessary to bring in extended family members to help with the decision and its execution. As mentioned before, only the young adult does not get to participate in the decisions the family is making.

Once the family selects a door, the therapist instructs them to commit to their choice for a minimum of one month. At that time, the therapist and the family can make a decision to continue with their course of action or select another.

DOOR 1—THE AUTHORITATIVE APPROACH

Ms Smith came alone to the first session. She tearfully stated that Jeff, her 20-year-old son, had assaulted her and her 17-year-old daughter, Ann. She said that Jeff had threatened them with a knife and had broken up their furniture. He refused to leave the house and find a place of his own. Jeff works sporadically as a laborer, quitting whenever confronted by a boss for his lackadaisical attitude.

Ms Smith and her husband had divorced five years previously. Jeff rarely contacts his father, who lives in a different state. His mother feels an overwhelming responsibility to help Jeff become an adult, and she blames herself and her divorce for his shortcomings. Ms Smith has tried to establish a life for herself through work and dating. When men arrive to take her out, however, Jeff insults them until they leave, acting more like a jealous husband than as a son. Ms Smith often ends up not going out as she fears that Jeff may destroy the house while she's gone.

When asked what she could do to stop Jeff's violent behavior, Ms Smith said her only option was to call her brother, a large man who worked in construction. Usually she just placated Jeff to keep him from getting out of control. Ms Smith pays most of his bills on their due date as Jeff often "forgets" to pay them. Although she does lecture Jeff about his responsibilities, her daughter, Ann, tells Ms Smith that she needs to be stricter, but she can never bring herself to take her daughter's advice. Ms Smith remarked that Ann did not fear Jeff the way she does and often confronts him on his behavior.

Jeff refused to attend therapy with his mother. When I contacted him by phone, Jeff said there was nothing wrong with him and, therefore, he did not want to come in for therapy. After speaking with Ms Smith and Jeff, I decided that the "doors" method might be helpful with the family. I presented the Let's Make a Deal format to Ms Smith and explained each of the choices. Ms Smith chose door #1, the authoritative approach, because she felt that her daughter would be upset with her if she didn't select that one. I asked permission to contact Ann by phone so that she could help her mother with the strategy.

Ms Smith returned home and announced her plan to Jeff. She said that she wanted his cooperation on three issues:

1. Any violence would result in an immediate phone call to Jeff's uncle.

2. Ms Smith would place Jeff's bills on the kitchen table and would leave them unopened.

3. Ms Smith would expect Jeff to look for work each day. A failure to look for work would result in Jeff's washing his own clothes, making his own meals, and spending his own money for gas and entertainment.

For the first week after the initial therapy session, Jeff tested his mother's new authoritative position, but she refused to cave in. During the second week of the intervention, Ann provoked Jeff by screaming at him, and he threw a knife at her. Ms Smith called me in hysterics. I commented that even though Jeff had been provoked by Ann, he still had acted violently, and so his uncle should be called. In addition, it was recommended that Ann also be disciplined if, under any circumstances, she provoked Jeff again. Ms Smith and Ann agreed to the new terms.

Other situations arose that tested Ms Smith's resolve. A bill for Jeff's car insurance arrived in the mail and Ms Smith became anxious and called the therapist. The three components of her agreement under door 1 were reviewed. She left the statement unopened on the table. On the last possible due date, Ms Smith received a frantic call from Jeff while at work. He wanted to know if the insurance company would accept cash from him. She assured him that it would and reminded him to get a receipt. Despite other incidents, Ms Smith managed to enforce her three primary issues, enlisting my support whenever necessary.

After three weeks, Ms Smith was able to have a male friend visit on a Sunday afternoon without incident. Later that week, Jeff called to say he had found a better-paying job with more hours. He told Ms Smith he loved her and then asked if she would have any objections to his moving in with a friend when he had saved enough money. She agreed that he needed to live his own life.

A six-month follow-up found Jeff living with his girlfriend and continuing in the same job. Ms Smith still dated the man she had invited to her home on that Sunday afternoon. Ann was attending college away from home.

DOOR 2—THE MAINTENANCE APPROACH

Mr. and Mrs. Jones came to the first session with their 19-year-old son, Robert, and their 12-year-old daughter, Susan. Since the age of 14, Robert had been hospitalized four times for psychiatric problems. The Jones family reported that Robert had violent temper tantrums, during which he would threaten to kill his father and would beat his fists against the wall. Robert, a husky 220-pound young man, sat apart from his family, staring at them with contempt. When asked to state his version of the problem, Robert became sullen and refused to talk.

Halfway into the first session, I asked everyone but Robert to leave the room. Robert said that he did not want to talk in front of his family and preferred to be seen alone. I asked Robert if he had any objections if his parents and sister also were seen by themselves, and he said no. The family was brought back to the session while Robert waited outside. I asked them for a detailed accounting of what happens when their son is violent. They described the following scenario.

> Robert becomes violent. Mrs. Jones confronts Robert in the
> midst of his violent episode. Robert blames his behavior on
> the fact that his father drinks too much and his mother
> doesn't give him enough love. Mr. Jones tries to intervene

and help his wife get control of Robert. Mrs. Jones then sides with her son, and together she and Robert verbally attack Mr. Jones until Robert leaves the house. Mr. and Mrs. Jones then argue about their respective treatment of Robert.

The Let's Make a Deal method seemed appropriate for the family. I described the plan, but the family showed little reaction to my presentation of the procedure. I asked them to decide on a choice in the week between sessions. When they returned, the family said they had not discussed the three choices, even though Robert had several violent episodes. The second session consisted of more complaints about Robert's behavior.

The family did not mention the choices when they came to the third session. I remarked that they were choosing door 2 by default, since they were still in the same predictable behavior pattern. I reiterated their habitual pattern: Mrs. Jones would confront Robert and then be protective of him in relation to his father; Mr. Jones would come to his wife's defense in a demeaning manner that would result in her changing her focus from Robert to attacking her husband; and Robert would insult both of his parents and then eventually leave the house. I asked the family if this accounting were accurate, and they agreed.

The family came to the fourth session extremely upset. They looked frustrated and begged me to do something about Robert's behavior. I once again went over the three choices available to the family, reminding them that the door they had selected, door 2, often resulted in frustration with no change in behavior. The family asked to have the other choices repeated and then chose door 1, the authoritative approach.

Without Robert present, we discussed the rules and consequences the family wished to enforce. They decided:

1. The parents would never oppose each other whenever an episode occurred.

2. If Robert cranked the stereo up to full volume, he would be given one warning before the power in the house was turned off.

3. If violence occurred, the police would be called.

During the first two days of the intervention, there were no incidents. Mrs. Jones called on the third day to relate that Robert had turned up the stereo to full volume. His sister, Susan, warned him that if he didn't turn it down, the power in the house would be turned off. After no response from Robert, Susan turned off the power. Robert became furious and started abusing his sister verbally. The parents stayed supportive of Susan and each other. When Robert began to destroy the furniture, Susan called the police. The police suggested that Mr. and Mrs. Jones not press charges this time, but should contact them if Robert became violent again. In that instance, Robert would be locked up.

This was clearly the turning point in the therapy, although there were other, minor incidents that the parents resolved. Robert found a job and decided to live with his girlfriend, 10 years his senior. When his relationship with her was not going well, Robert called me for help.

DOOR 3—THE UNCONDITIONAL-LOVE APPROACH

Mr. Patrick called about his son Mack and wanted an appointment that same day. He and his wife arrived at the session looking desperate and asking for answers. Mr. Patrick indicated that they had previously attended therapy for over five years and did not wish to undertake it again at this time. He only wanted to meet with me once so he could take a clear position with his son.

Mr. and Mrs. Patrick described Mack as a 24-year-old bartender, sometimes bum. He slept all day, went to work at 5 o'clock if he felt like it, and partied all night. Both the mother and father felt that their affluence financed Mack's hedonistic existence. Mack dated beautiful women and seemed unconcerned about other parts of his life. He laughed when his parents spoke to him about responsibility.

When presented with the three doors, the Patricks said there was only one practical choice for them, door 3. They felt that they had no control over Mack and so wouldn't be effective with door 1. Door 2 was out of the question, since they wanted immediate action.

Together we planned out the strategy. I told the parents they would have to sacrifice their life each day to make Mack feel comfortable and loved. This could include telling him how much they cared about him, having his favorite meals ready whenever he wanted them, changing the TV channel for him, and suggesting that he not work because it might be too stressful. They should give Mack money for entertainment and call him from work to see if he needed anything. The Patricks agreed to the plan, but said they did not wish to set up another appointment, as they could execute the technique on their own. After two months I contacted the Patricks to see what had happened. They reported that Mack was currently living in Atlanta, working as a stockbroker by day and a bartender at night. They said that on the fourth day of the intervention, Mack decided his life was too boring, and he needed a change. He called a friend in Atlanta and learned of the stockbroker position. Two weeks later, he packed his bags and moved to Georgia.

The Let's Make a Deal method is highly successful in working with young adults who refuse to leave home, but is also effective in any illusion of control situation where the client or family asks a therapist for help, but refuses to relinquish control. The strategy allows the locus of control to remain with the family or client, despite the therapist's providing concise action plans with predictable outcomes. The therapist assumes a supportive role, reinforcing whatever decision the family makes rather than directing the therapy. This maximizes the family's emotional investment in their choice, while minimizing their opposition to the therapist. The plan also consolidates a power base within the family away from the person who previously wielded the most control, and increases consistency among family members.

The Let's Make a Deal strategy provides a vehicle for change without the therapist's appearing to initiate or control the action. It is the therapist who constructs the final illusion, however, since the family's choice is within the confines of the intervention.

13

TOGETHER AND APART

There are times when one member of a couple will present for therapy, asking for help in terminating the relationship but refusing to include the partner. Therapists are placed in an awkward situation and must make the decision to accept the client's position, change it, or refuse to see the client. Some systems of therapy advocate against seeing the individual, as therapist participation would be a form of collusion against the absent partner. Other approaches recommend that the therapist take an active stand against the separation, as it would be ethically wrong to promote the dissolution of a marriage at the request of one member. Most systems actively encourage the client to bring the absent partner into the session, as well as any other relevant family members, to try and save the marriage before working toward an adaptive termination of the relationship. If clients refuse to include their partners, usually because they fear revealing their intent before reaching a firm decision, the therapist sees the clients individually to help them make an empowered decision.

If the choice is made to see the client alone, the therapist often finds himself or herself enmeshed in an illusion of control situation generated by the client's ambivalence. The client has essentially asked the therapist for help in making a decision he or she has been unable to make. Despite asking for assistance, such clients create obstacles for the therapy in much the same way that they have placed obstructions in the exit from their relationship. The clients punctuate their remarks to the therapist with questions about "why" they have a problem or "why" they are unable to leave. Like other illusion of control clients, they want explanations, but not suggestions, from the therapist.

Clients in violent, pathological, or unsatisfying relationships frequently appeal for help because they are in desperate situations. But despite their difficulties, they often refuse the therapist's input when offered. The clients reject the therapist's suggestions in the same way that they discount their own good reasons for leaving. In the same vein, the clients typically regale the therapist with horror stories about their marriages, but if the therapist comments critically about their partners, the clients become angry at the therapist and supportive of their spouses. The situation is analogous to what happens when law enforcement officers are called to deal with a domestic situation, in that the officers are often assaulted by the victim if they attempt to interfere with the perpetrator. The therapist is not alone in receiving approbation from the clients. The clients also turn on themselves, wondering what type of person would remain in a terrible or loveless marriage.

In these cases, as in all cases, the therapist can only take as much action as the client allows. The client's illusion of control often entices the therapist into a role of co-conspirator, only to find that the client's own participation has vaporized. It is more useful for the therapist to resist such clients' overtures, encouraging them to keep control of the process in a way that allows them to resolve both their ambivalence and their problems.

METHOD

In the following section an approach is described that can be used by therapists in situations in which a client is ambivalent about terminating a relationship and resistant to direct suggestions. The technique is predicated on the idea that the ambivalence suspends the client between two positions, keeping the client from either investing in the relationship or ending it. By leaving control of the decision with the clients, but providing them with impetus to strengthen the relationship with their partners, the therapist enables them to break their impasse and resolve their problems.

The technique should be tried after direct suggestions to help clients in their quest to terminate their relationships have been repeatedly rejected. The therapist defers to the clients, stating that perhaps they are right that they are not ready to leave their partners. The therapist then asks the clients to describe an ideal relationship. They are told that they should include the desired level of affection, work behavior, sexual relations, attitudes toward children—essentially anything that is important to them. Once a client has detailed the list, the therapist asks the client to look at how his or her own behavior differs from the described relationship. The client is not allowed to shift the blame or responsibility to the partner. The therapist points out that as the other person is not present, that person can't help to change the situation. The client is to look at only those ways his or her own behavior differs from the ideal.

Once the discrepancies are noted, the therapist suggests that clients adopt their idyllic postures for a month. They should behave toward their partners as if they had the perfect relationship. At the end of that time, clients can reevaluate their situations and decide whether to stay or leave.

Clients usually accept the idea, especially if the therapist frames it as a way for them to make sure that they have tried every possible means of making their marriage work before they leave. Some clients will balk at the prospect of being pleasant with an abusive or difficult spouse, but the therapist should make clear there is no other way to address the problem at this time. If the client returns to the idea that it is the partner's actions and not the client's that need to change, the therapist should repeat that it is useless to ask the partner to act differently since the person is not present; moreover, the client has never been successful in the past with getting the partner to change his or her behavior.

The strength of the technique is that it allows control to remain with clients in that they have designated the target behaviors and will be the only ones responsible for evaluating their outcome. By encouraging them to commit to a course of action and move toward their partner, the impasse of their ambivalence will be broken.

DAPHNE

Daphne appeared for therapy, equally upset about her marriage and her inability to end it. She had been married to Pete for 14 years. Although they were happy at the beginning, things changed when Pete began to use alcohol and marijuana heavily. Daphne's main criticism of his addictions was that they caused Pete to withdraw, so he never wanted to spend time with either her or their 12-year-old daughter. Sex was an ordeal since Pete was either unmotivated or reeked of drugs and alcohol. Seven years earlier, Daphne had engaged in an affair with a younger man because he gave her the attention she craved. She said she felt flattered by the involvement and she was crushed when he dropped her. Daphne and Pete tried marriage therapy shortly thereafter, but when the therapist dismissed Pete's drinking as inconsequential, Daphne wouldn't return.

Daphne maintained that she desperately wanted to leave Pete but had never found the courage. She held no confidence in her ability to make good decisions. From the time she was a little girl, Daphne's parents had been highly critical of her. When she mentioned to them that she was considering leaving Pete, her mother told Daphne that any problems in the marriage were probably of her own doing, and so she should start treating her husband better.

Daphne's friends were a different story. Because Pete never wanted to go anywhere or do anything, Daphne had developed a strong core of companions, many of whom had never met her husband. All of her friends were pushing Daphne to get out of her marriage and make a new life for herself. Daphne agreed with them but was terrified of ending up alone.

Daphne refused to consider bringing Pete into therapy with her. She told me that if he attended, she would never get the courage to leave him. What she wanted out of therapy was for me to help her become strong enough to take the steps she wanted to take. I expressed my reservations about being able to accomplish her goal under the circumstances, but agreed to try.

For several sessions, I listened to Daphne complain about Pete. Daphne, however, was not willing to listen to me about anything. I realized that a direct approach would not have any chance of successfully resolving either Daphne's marriage or her ambivalence, and that a more indirect intervention was required. I began by sympathizing with Daphne about her dilemma and said the situation was overwhelming me as well. Perhaps, I said, since Daphne couldn't leave Pete, she should work to make her marriage an ideal one. I asked Daphne to list all of the qualities she would like to see in their relationship. When she finished, I suggested that she needed to recreate her marriage to Pete in a way that was acceptable to her. According to her list, Daphne wanted to spend a lot of time with Pete and pursue activities together. The couple would engage in an active sex life and enjoy time with their daughter. Daphne and Pete would do spontaneous, fun things for each other and be very affectionate and loving. I suggested that Daphne try to accomplish this in her marriage, giving it a good try for one month. Only then would she know if her marriage could be saved.

Daphne demurred, saying she didn't think these changes were possible because of Pete's addictions. I told Daphne she could only be responsible for her part of the process. Since Pete weren't here, we couldn't ask or demand that he do the same. At least Daphne would have the satisfaction of behaving the way she thought was appropriate, and perhaps her actions would inspire Pete. Daphne finally agreed to try because the current form of her marriage was torturous, and since she couldn't find the strength to leave Pete, anything had to be an improvement.

Two weeks later, Daphne returned to therapy, stating that it was impossible to continue this course of action. She said that she was going crazy sitting in front of the television with Pete, since this was the only activity he was willing to share. Daphne's attempts to have sex with her husband made her sick. In addition, Pete was so inappropriate when interacting with their daughter that Daphne was unhappy about subjecting the girl to his incompetence. Daphne had decided to terminate her marriage since she realized there was nothing she could do to save it. She said that she hoped she had the strength of her conviction.

I suggested Daphne set a deadline for informing Pete of her decision. That date could be a day, a week, or a year later. If she did not talk to Pete when that time arrived, she must abandon the idea of leaving him for at least another year. During those 12 months, Daphne was not to complain to anyone about Pete's behavior or to consider leaving him. She should think of it as a one-year vacation from making her decision, a holiday from worrying. Daphne decided to tell Pete before her next birthday. As the date approached, she wavered, but mustered the courage to talk to her husband. Daphne was surprised at how well the conversation went. Both partners agreed that the marriage was over, and they decided to consult an independent therapist to help them separate amicably and establish custody parameters.

In an interesting postscript to the case, the mediation therapist ignored the suggestions in my referral and the couple's wish to divorce, and attempted to reinstate the marriage. Daphne was able to hold firm to her decision despite the pressure. Because her individual therapy had been structured in such a way that Daphne was able to use her control to move past her ambivalence, she maintained her commitment even when faced with criticism. A two-year follow-up found Daphne living with an indulgent boyfriend who got along well with her daughter. The couple planned to marry the next month. Pete was working hard to overcome his addictions and was being more responsible with his daughter.

CARRIE

For two months, Carrie and her husband, Ed, had attended marital therapy with little success. Carrie was a 52-year-old professional woman with a responsible government job. Ed was a 45-year-old blue collar worker who seemed to go out of his way to act foolishly during the sessions. Both Carrie and Ed were on their third marriage. Although the couple said they were anxious to make their relationship of five years work, neither was participating constructively in the therapeutic process.

Ed and Carrie's primary complaint with their marriage was their arguing, which often escalated into violence. Ed had beaten Carrie with his fists; Carrie had shot at Ed with a gun. The arguments frequently began by Ed's criticizing something his wife had done or had failed to do. When Carrie defended herself, Ed would attack her character and make fun of her status. Ed was obsessed with the fact that Carrie made more money than he did and that she had a college degree.

My initial attempts at therapy focused on raising Ed's status in the marriage. Any suggestion, however, provoked a round of disagreements, with Ed contemptuous and Carrie defending both herself and me. All efforts to exercise control proved futile, and I was generally relegated to the role of audience for their altercations. Once the couple finished arguing with each other, they would turn on me, demanding a solution to their problem.

One afternoon, Ed was called away on a work project, and Carrie came to therapy by herself. She told me that they were not sure that they should continue in therapy since their problems weren't being resolved. Carrie became tearful and told me that she really wanted to leave Ed, that although she loved him, their arguments overwhelmed her. She begged me to give her some idea of how to terminate the relationship.

Carrie countered each suggestion I gave her with an argument. At the end of her last dismissal, I agreed with Carrie that leaving Ed seemed too difficult at this time. I asked her to consider all of the things she could do to make her marriage be everything she wanted. Carrie said that most of their relationship was perfect, except for the arguing. I asked Carrie if she could imagine any way to avoid the fights. She observed that the fighting always occurred when she defended herself. The only way she could see stopping their fights would be to agree with everything Ed said. I suggested that the idea might be worth a try, since she didn't seem to have the strength to leave right now. Carrie replied that she wasn't sure it would work, and that she also didn't think it would be fair to agree with Ed when she thought he was wrong. I pointed out that Carrie hadn't been able to convince Ed about the rightness of her position in the past, and that perhaps it would be more fun to see how far Ed would go in defending a point he knew to be wrong. I congratulated Carrie on the ingenuity of her solution and suggested that her stance might actually convince Ed to change his attitude. Carrie agreed to try, and to come alone to the following session to report whether or not she was successful.

At her next appointment, Carrie reported a remarkable turnaround in the relationship. All week Ed would be poised, waiting for an argument, and all he got was agreement. Carrie expressed surprise at how easy it had been to be conciliatory, and said that the decrease in arguing had more than compensated her for keeping her opinions to herself. A particularly amusing episode had occurred while they were watching the TV game show "Jeopardy." Ed gave his opinion of what the correct question should be for Final Jeopardy, and Carrie agreed with him, even though she knew it was incorrect. When the correct question was announced, Carrie suggested that the show had made a mistake since anything on which she and Ed both agreed couldn't be wrong. They laughed about writing the show's producer to correct them, and the whole event had developed into a sweet, private joke.

Ed phoned to thank me for helping his wife and their marriage. He said that he realized they had given me a hard time, and he appreciated the final result. Ed wasn't sure what Carrie and I were working on, but he knew he didn't have to struggle so much when they were together.

When Carrie came in for her last session, she stated that Ed no longer was so critical of her, so she rarely had to agree with him when she didn't mean it. Whenever she felt that they were slipping toward an argument, however, she returned to a more conciliatory attitude. Once the tension between them disappeared, Ed would often admit that he was wrong and would support Carrie's view.

ETHAN

Ethan was distraught. Two months earlier, he had terminated a relationship with Louise, his lover of two years. When he moved out of their apartment into a place of his own, Louise began to harass him. She called him constantly and showed up at his new apartment building at any hour of the day or night. If Ethan didn't answer the door, Louise would shout obscenities into his letter slot, much to the amusement and horror of his neighbors. One of the most embarrassing moments occurred when Ethan and a group of people from his office went to a charity benefit at a local art gallery. As he was talking to one of his female coworkers, Louise charged into the party and slapped the woman, calling her a home wrecker and a whore. Louise continued to hurl obscenities until a security guard dragged her away from the function.

I suggested some ways in which Ethan might deal with the situation, but he rejected each of them. He was afraid of upsetting Louise any further because she threatened to take action against him at work if he did. I commented that Louise was acting in a dangerous manner, and he should really consider taking legal steps against her. Ethan said he was desperate enough to do just that, but that he feared Louise's reaction if he did bring charges. Louise had told Ethan that she was prepared to announce to everyone that he was a child molester and a coke head if he ever tried to have her arrested. Ethan did not want to have to defend himself against even false charges. Louise was ruining his life, and he didn't have the power to stop her.

I agreed with Ethan that he was helpless to stop Louise. I suggested that since he was effectively being held hostage, he might as well make it overt. As Ethan wasn't capable of stopping Louise, he might as well give in to her. He'd be miserable, but at least he'd still have a job and stay out of jail. I told Ethan to consider his return to Louise a vacation from the harassment. Perhaps after the rest, he'd feel stronger and be able to follow through on another idea.

Louise was startled with Ethan's reappearance and suspicious as to why he had resumed their relationship. She immediately asked Ethan if he still loved her. Ethan admitted that he had come back only because he wanted a more peaceful life. Seeing Louise was preferable to being tormented on a constant basis. Louise also inquired if Ethan were prepared to resume their sexual relationship. Ethan told her he'd do his best, but while his spirit was willing, his flesh might be weak.

Louise went berserk. She told Ethan he was humiliating her by his presence. Ethan insisted he was not trying to injure Louise in any way but only wanted to lead a noncontentious life. He explained that he was tired of looking around to see if she were stalking him or going to threaten him. Ethan told Louise it was easier to spend time with her than to worry constantly about what she might be plotting. Louise began screaming at Ethan and threw him out of her house.

When Ethan appeared for the next therapy session, he was relieved, but concerned. While no longer worried about Louise's stalking him, he was anxious to learn how he had contributed to the situation in the first place. He asked if I would help him look at the ways he treated women, because Ethan suspected he had contributed to Louise's rage by his own behavior. The remainder of our work together centered on helping Ethan with some of his underlying issues regarding relationships.

Many clients present the illusion of control to a therapist because they are stuck in a relationship and are unable to move either toward or away from their partners. The client begs the therapist to help him or her separate from a bad situation, but the therapist's suggestions are countered or ignored as the client struggles with his or her own ambivalence. The method detailed in this chapter demonstrates how helping clients move toward their partners, while allowing them to keep control of their issues, often alleviates the impasse that prevents a successful resolution of the relationship. Once the inertia is overcome, clients are free to determine the direction they want the final resolution to take. Additionally, because the therapist works toward improving the relationship, the therapist can feel less guilty about colluding with the client against the nonparticipating member of the couple. The intervention gives the relationship every chance to succeed before the client makes a decision.

14

SUPERVISION

Control dynamics become even more complex in the context of one therapist's supervising another. A supervisor may be presented with varying levels of control from supervisees who themselves are handling a variety of control issues regarding their clients. Supervisors who work within the auspices of an agency, or even a structured therapeutic model, have a level of control above them as well, and need to factor policy or philosophy issues into the equation. To be effective in this multitiered system, supervisors must understand the control dimensions on each level and structure their help in a way that fosters the supervisees' development while meeting the needs of the clients and organizational structure.

The supervisee's control pattern should be the initial and primary focus for the supervisor. Client issues are irrelevant if a supervisor is unable to communicate ways of dealing with those problems to a supervisee in a way the supervisee will accept. While the supervisor has an obligation to both the client and the agency, this responsibility is discharged through the supervisee. The supervisor's ability to understand and use the control pattern of the supervisee becomes essential to successful resolution at all levels.

In an ideal world, supervisees come to supervision ready to expand their skills and to gain new insights from a supervisor they admire and trust. As in therapy, situations are rarely so pure. Some supervisees are ordered to see a specific supervisor involuntarily, others have theoretical orientations or personality characteristics that make them suspicious of a particular supervisor, and some are unable to relinquish control to another person in any context. Supervisors typically meet these challenges with the same variety of unsuccessful techniques used with noncooperative clients. Some supervisors try to impose their will on a stubborn supervisee, others attempt to dazzle the supervisee with brilliance. In the most difficult cases, the supervisory relationship is terminated out of frustration. If, however, supervisors position themselves according to the supervisees' control issues, there can be a more successful and pleasurable resolution to the supervision.

TOTAL CONTROL

There are supervisees who come to supervision looking for answers. This is particularly true in those cases where the supervisor is regarded as an expert. Therapists in a crisis situation also approach supervision willing to accept what the supervisor has to say. Because they are stymied by a difficult case or an absence of solutions, they welcome the supervisor's help in resolving their difficulties. Beginning therapists, or those learning a new system, frequently fall into this category, although experienced therapists will also give total control to a supervisor if their client's problems are sufficiently extreme or the supervisor has master status.

In the context of total control, the supervisor is able to take an authoritarian stance and give direct, specific suggestions to the supervisee. The advice can focus on both the client's needs and the supervisee's professional goals. For instance, a supervisor might suggest that a therapist ask a particular family member to attend the client's next session. The explicit goal of the advice is to better address the client's presenting and underlying problems, while the implicit purpose might be to expand the supervisee's skills in handling family interactions.

As mentioned in Chapter 1, total control situations place a high level of responsibility in the hands of the therapist who is holding the power. This is true of supervisory cases as well, and a supervisor given total control must exercise discretion and work to empower their supervisee. Supervisees must be encouraged to learn from their mentors, but should also be pushed to develop a style uniquely their own.

The problem is exacerbated in situations where the supervisor is a master. Legions of therapists have gone through training programs, only to emerge as copies of their teacher. They not only imitate the therapeutic style of their mentor, but also their teacher's appearance, style of dress, and facial expressions. Unfortunately, what works for the master often fails for the student. This is especially true if the therapist lacks some vital element that made the process flourish in the hands of their teacher. I once watched a student of Carl Whitaker's at work, trying desperately to be provocative with a client. The therapist was cold and arrogant, and the technique failed abominably, whereas Whitaker, with his engaging warmth, would probably have pulled it off.

Total control supervisees willingly absorb all suggestions made by their supervisor, but they often lack the discrimination to know what is relevant. Jay Haley used to complain that students would often record, as gospel, humorous remarks he made, rather than laugh at the joke or catch the sarcasm. I can remember sitting at the Family Therapy Institute, watching the woman next to me write down every intervention mentioned across a one-year period. She conscientiously recorded every detail of cases presented, and by the end of the training, she had compiled a catalog of master techniques for use with her clients. Unfortunately she never paid attention to why a particular intervention was being used or what the therapist was trying to accomplish during a session, and so her transcriptions were not likely to be useful.

Total control supervision is also a problem when the supervisor is incompetent. Supervisee and clients suffer alike at the hands of experts who actually have no idea of what they are doing. One rural clinic put a first-year graduate psychiatrist in charge of the clinical staff because of his medical status. Senior therapists at the center ignored his direction, but the newer practitioners hung on his every word. Their yielding of control to a supervisor without experience had some disastrous consequences for the clients in their care. Total control supervision can promote growth and success for everyone involved, but only when it is handled judiciously and responsibly by both the supervisor and supervisee.

PARTIAL CONTROL

The majority of supervisory interactions fall in the category of partial control. Many therapists have confidence in their own abilities but are interested in pursuing alternate approaches or expanding their repertoire of skills. They are willing to be cooperative as long as they value what the supervisor has to say. If the supervisor fails to meet their expectations, however, the therapists are confident enough in their own beliefs to challenge the suggestions given.

Therapy under partial control conditions can be a productive, collaborative effort if each member respects the opinions and skills of the other. Control shifts back and forth, from supervisor to supervisee, and both contribute to a successful outcome. The interaction yields positive benefits for both parties, and there are transitions in power rather than struggles for control.

Sometimes his or her theoretical orientation can block a therapist from accepting a supervisor's instructions at first pass. If a suggestion seems foreign or antithetical, a therapist may resist the supervisor's direction. Supervisors must be as patient with their supervisees as they are with clients who get anxious about shifting out of habitual ways of behaving. Pressure to adopt a new approach can be delayed until a more propitious moment, or until underlying issues can be used to hook a supervisee into trying a plan.

Dan, an experienced psychodynamic therapist, came to me for supervision. He wanted input about a case involving a 23-year-old psychiatric patient who lived at home. This young man spent his time doing good deeds for everyone in his family, as well as for strangers, but was unwilling to do anything for himself. Dan's theoretical orientation led him to believe that the client was in need of "parenting." I suggested that the case might better be handled as a family issue. I asked Dan to involve the young man's family in the next session, where he could reframe the client as a religious figure who gave to others at the expense of himself. Dan resisted the idea of asking the family to participate because he said that he didn't think it would help his client gain insight into his issues. After several resisted attempts at convincing Dan to try my approach, I shifted my position and focused on different ways that Dan could better "parent" his client. When Dan returned a month later, he reported good success with one of the strategies and asked me how he might extend the intervention to include the client's family. By yielding to Dan's theoretical beliefs and using his language to discuss the client, I circumvented a struggle for control while generating enough credibility to allow him eventually to shift his position.

Sometimes a therapist gives only partial control to a supervisor because of the therapist's confusion about a client. As the supervisor attempts to clarify the situation, the therapist realizes he or she has not understood the underlying dynamics of the case well enough to present them in a comprehensible fashion. The impasse in supervision is caused by poor analysis, not by noncompliance. Evaluating why the supervisor's suggestions seem incorrect forces the therapist to reexamine, and more adequately explain, the client's problem.

In cases where therapists are not able to choose their supervisors, they often adopt a "wait and see" attitude, withholding total compliance until the supervisors have prove themselves competent. The situation is similar to that of a new client's apprehension about an unknown therapist. The client is hesitant to engage with the therapist until the therapist has demonstrated that he or she is trustworthy. In the same way, unless a supervisor has received good press from colleagues or is well known, the supervisee is reluctant to accept the supervisor's judgment until confidence is established.

I received a phone call from Trudy seeking my supervision. Trudy was in a master's program in social work and needed supervised field placement to finish her degree. Her first call had been to the Family Therapy Institute, which had recommended me as a potential supervisor.

Trudy had a lot of questions during the initial interview. Social work was her third career; her first had been as an actress in England and her second was as a mother. Trudy expressed uncertainty about how a 30-year-old man with no children could possibly teach her, a 58-year-old woman with grown children, about families. I told her I probably couldn't and offered her some ideas as to where else she might go for field placement. When Trudy protested that the Institute had specifically referred her to me, I suggested we try to work on several cases together, and if it didn't work out, I'd help her find an older supervisor. Trudy agreed to the plan, but indicated that it wasn't only my age and childlessness that bothered her. She had read a lot of material by Haley and Erickson while in school, and she made it clear she would much rather have been assigned either of them as a supervisor.

Trudy began her field placement and quickly demonstrated a flair for therapy. For the first month of her supervision, I would preface any comment I made to Trudy with the words, "Jay Haley would . . ." or "Milton Erickson has been known to . . .". I never suggested what I would do, but only stated what more experienced and famous therapists would try. Finally, after several weeks of this, Trudy asked me what I, and not some famous person, would do in a particular situation. She had gained sufficient respect by watching me work to value my opinion. By taking a yielding posture, and using Trudy's underlying issue of wanting a famous person to supervise her, I was able to overcome her initial wariness and obtain status as her supervisor.

NO CONTROL

Some therapists do not give the supervisor any control over the supervisory relationship. This can occur if the supervisee feels superior to the supervisor because of education or experience. It is also seen in situations where the therapist has been assigned to a particular therapist against his or her will or because an agency or regulatory body is insisting on an increased level of supervision. The therapist in this situation is similar to an involuntary client, as he or she needs to comply with the assignment, but has no desire to participate in the process. Other therapists refuse to yield control because they see the supervisor's theoretical orientation as conflictual with or antithetical to their own.

Supervisees also might not give control to a supervisor if some aspect of their personalities prohibits them from doing so. In some cases, lack of cooperation is produced by anxiety about or insecurity over performance, feelings that are exacerbated during live supervision. Supervisees become so distraught that they are unable to process any of the supervisor's instructions. Their withholding of control is more a product of immobility due to anxiety than it is a willful disregard of instructions.

When I first arrived at the Family Therapy Institute, I was a 28-year-old social worker with little experience in working with difficult families. I was scheduled to see my first client, a 25-year-old heroin addict, who was being accompanied to the session by his brother, his mother, and his grandmother. In discussing the case with my supervisor, Cloe Madanes, I realized I was so nervous about her and the other trainees watching me from behind the one-way mirror that I didn't think I could even conduct the session. Despite the fact that we had prepared extensively for the family, I knew I wouldn't be able to execute the plan, or even stop my voice from cracking, because I was so nervous about being observed. I asked if I could see the family myself, with no one watching, or that perhaps someone else could take over the case and I could learn from their example.

Cloe realized she had no control over my anxiety regarding supervision. She told me that the heroin addict and his family were going to be so difficult for me that I would have no time to be anxious about her or the other trainees. Her statement redirected my anxiety away from the supervisory situation, of which I was highly fearful, to worrying about the client, a matter I had indicated was less traumatic.

The session went well. I focused on our plan of enlisting the family to help the addict monitor his drug use through regular urinalysis, something the client had refused to do on his own. Cloe rarely interjected comments during that first session, allowing me to feel more relaxed about being observed. During subsequent meetings with the family, when I was more confident about being watched, Cloe increased her level of input concerning the case.

Insecurity certainly can affect supervisees, but they also might refuse control to a supervisor because of a need to demonstrate their own importance. The therapist sees any suggestion by the supervisor as an assault on his or her competence that must be repelled. No matter how constructively the advice is framed, the supervisee contemptuously rejects the help as unnecessary. Supervisors often become frustrated in this no control situation, and either try to coerce the supervisee into following their directions or terminate the supervision out of anger. As in other no control interactions, the supervisor is better off redirecting the therapist, as described above, or exaggerating the problem, as in the following situation.

Brad was hired by our agency fresh out of school. He came highly recommended by all of his psychology professors, and was also well regarded by the special school where he had done his internship. Brad was very engaging and attractive, and it was clear from the beginning that he was used to smoothing any difficulties with his charm and wit.

Brad was assigned to me for supervision. He deferred our getting together for the first two months, saying he needed to get his feet wet before he could even think of swimming. He finally arranged a time for a supervisory session. I asked him what he wanted to work on, what his goals were for our meeting. Brad began by describing a case in which he was currently involved. After he finished, I complimented him on his presentation and suggested some areas he might pursue. Brad countered each idea, regaling me with reasons why his way would work better. After a few rounds of this interchange, Brad terminated our session, saying that he had another appointment and needed to leave.

Supervision proceeded in much this way for six months. Brad was not interested in any of the books, articles, or videotapes I suggested for him, and while deferential and polite to me, he accepted no idea or strategy I put forth during our sessions. Brad refused to have live supervision and never accepted an invitation to watch me, or any of my other supervisees, work. The situation was clearly one of no control, and any efforts on my part to actively supervise Brad were stifled.

When Brad next appeared for supervision, I told him our situation was futile. I said that he clearly did not need supervision and did not want supervision, and that I supported him in his stand. I added that he should be confident enough in his feelings to challenge the organization's requirement for supervision. I suggested he write a letter to the manager, explaining why, since he had so much recent educational training, he did not need any further input. Certainly, with his year of internship so fresh, he did not require any other guidance at this time. I likened Brad to a glass of water, brimming full. His mind was so filled with his own ideas and knowledge that if anyone tried to introduce another concept, everything would come spilling out. I suggested he let the manager know when he was less full, so that I might be of better service.

Brad seemed very upset. He said that at this point in a new job, he would rather not make an issue of it. I assured him that I would support him in his right to determine when he needed supervision, and that length of career shouldn't be the determining factor. I pointed out that I had some 20 years of experience but felt I benefited from collaboration and supervision. Who was to say when in a career supervision was the most useful? Brad was quiet for a moment, and then mentioned a current case with which he was having a problem. He described the situation and asked for my advice. I assured him that the difficulty was one he could resolve easily for himself. Brad agreed that he might be able to figure it out, but stated that he would really appreciate my input. I suggested some areas he might address. Brad thanked me for my ideas and said he would try them out during his next session with the client.

ILLUSION OF CONTROL

Some therapists appear for supervision begging for help with a difficult case, but are unable to carry out any suggestions the supervisor makes. Their despair may be a product of an unwieldy case load containing a large number of difficult clients whom they have been unable to help. Sometimes their inability to follow suggestions may be linked to an unwillingness to change their current situation, since they need the supervisor to appreciate how miserable and overburdened they are. Their helplessness might also be real, in that they have been so poorly trained or prepared for their current position that their inability to fix their client's problems has led to an expectation that they will never be able to do so.

A supervisor must also be conscious of whether a supervisee's helplessness is related in a metaphorically hierarchical way to his or her clients. It might be that the therapist's illusion of control in supervision is a product of the client's similar behavior to the supervisee during therapy. Alternatively, a therapist who offers illusion of control to a supervisor might actually be seeking similar qualities in his or her clients. In either case, the supervisor, supervisee, and client become entangled in a "game-playing interaction," with everyone asking for help and no one able to act effectively.

As in other illusion of control situations, a supervisor meets poor success by offering direct suggestions, but can effect some movement by encouraging therapists to use their control to achieve resolution of their problems. The supervisor can suggest that supervisees pay attention to what makes them feel more or less desperate with clients, or can offer a limited number of concrete alternatives from which the therapists can choose their own solutions to the problem. At no point should the supervisor attempt to rescue therapists or belittle the desperateness of the situation, as this would reinstate the control issues and provoke them into proving how helpless they actually are.

I was approached at a community mental health meeting by a colleague who wanted some input into a case. Sarah described the client as a 25-year-old successful businessman who presented for help with public speaking. Ironically, the man spent his entire sessions talking, especially complaining about the preferential treatment his younger bipolar brother received from their parents. Sarah, who was normally an active therapist, had not been able to interject more than a word into their conversations. She was unable to discuss the possibility of bringing in other family members, or even to set goals for the therapy, because the client wouldn't let her interrupt his monolog. The client had seen two other therapists before seeing Sarah. He complained to her that they never let him talk enough to fully explain his problem.

I gave Sarah some ideas about things to try, but she refused to consider them. Sarah told me I didn't understand how horrible this had been for her, and that it was impossible to imagine how frustrating this man was. I suggested that she bring in the client for live supervision, but she refused, saying she would not be able even to voice the suggestion to him. I told Sarah that she was in an extremely serious predicament, and that she could only hope to resolve it by collecting more information. I suggested that she not even attempt to talk during the next session, but spend the time writing down everything her client had to say for the first 50 minutes of the session. The next five minutes could be spent in silence while she checked her notes. Her client would be told that the last five minutes of the session would consist of her asking him questions so as to clarify his information. Sarah could continue the process until she had enough data to resolve the problem.

Sarah called to tell me that her client had agreed to the plan. He had difficulty talking for the entire 50 minutes, but when he was at a loss for words, Sarah maintained her silence and studied her notes until he began speaking again. After three sessions, her client reported feeling much better, and said that he had even successfully made a

presentation at a sales meeting. Sarah told me she had no
idea why her client was doing so well, but she was happy
about his progress. I laughingly suggested that she had
been such a good audience that he had overcome any fear
of speaking in front of one.

Sarah and her client had actually constructed a two-tiered illusion of
control situation. He refused to listen to her suggestions, and she
rejected all of mine. The intervention allowed her to stop struggling
against my ideas while permitting her client to stop fighting against
hers. Sarah was able to direct her desire for activity toward gathering
information. Her client was given permission and encouragement to
engage in behavior he was exhibiting anyway, and by allowing him to
retain control, he was able to resolve his problems.

Supervision produces the same control issues as seen between therapists and clients. Additionally, the supervisor must deal with cooperation and resistance from other hierarchical levels. A balance must be
achieved that meets the needs of clients, therapists, organizations, and
the supervisors themselves. By applying the principles of the transpositional approach, the supervisor can produce beneficial outcomes for
clients while helping the supervisee to develop professionally.

15

EXTENDING THE PLAN

In the previous chapters, the transpositional template was applied to control issues between therapists and clients. The theory also can be applied, however, in any interpersonal situation, and the use of appropriate hooks, levers, and tools is as useful in a business negotiation as in the treatment room. By understanding the control dynamics of a situation, any individual can position himself or herself in such a way as to maximize positive outcomes and diminish frustration.

Therapists are frequently asked for advice outside the therapeutic domain. Friends and family members, colleagues and secretaries, may approach therapists at a party, on the telephone, or in the hall, looking for expert advice or insight. Because therapists are used to functioning in a helping mode, they try not to respond rudely, but most are aware of the risk of proffering an opinion outside the therapeutic contract. Some therapists refuse assistance, insisting the person seek an unbiased view from another therapist. Others give basic, logical advice and then avoid further contact with that person concerning the individual's personal issues.

The transpositional model can be a useful structure for providing advice at a distance. Therapists can inquire about the control dynamics of a situation and give general suggestions about how a person could approach the problem. For instance, if a coworker is looking for help regarding a son's staying out on weekends without calling, a therapist can help the person ascertain his or her level of control over the son's behavior and suggest appropriate positions that can be taken in that context, without discussing specifics of family dynamics or offering concrete interventions. Usually, the presentation of ideas within the structure of the model can be used to help the individual clarify an approach he or she may want to take, without engaging the therapist directly in the problem.

FRIENDS AND RELATIVES

Therapists are often besieged with questions from friends and family members who want help with difficulties. They tug at the therapist, begging for advice, and are resistant to efforts that try to redirect them to another, less personally involved "expert." At times their persistence may be driven by the allure of getting free services, but usually it is a product of their immense trust in someone they know and love, or a reluctance to expose their issues to a stranger. No matter how loudly a therapist proclaims ethical or individual misgivings, the relative or friend persists in asking for just a minute of time and takes rejection as a personal affront.

In these situations, therapists who want to be helpful can use the issue of control as a means for discussing the problem. By "educating" the friend or family member in stances they might wish to take, the therapist can avoid becoming enmeshed in the details of the situation, and yet still be helpful. This, of course, assumes that the person asking for help is not involving the therapist in control dynamics of his or her own, and is actually planning to follow the therapist's suggestions. The scenario becomes considerably more complex if a relative begs for help, but because of issues in the relationship with the therapist, then argues with any idea that is presented. The therapist, in this situation, must deal with two levels of control, and any hope of achieving positive resolution of the presented problem will depend on handling both with skill. The therapist gets caught between the "rock" of the familial relationship, in which the therapist is over-involved, and the "hard place" of the relative's problem, in which the therapist is underinvolved. Resolving this sort of situation is not likely. A considerably better outcome can be achieved in cases where a friend or family member not only asks for help, but is willing to accept it.

Tom, a childhood friend, called me from another state. After 16 years of an unhappy marriage, he had finally decided to get a divorce. Because of their three children,

Tom was anxious to resolve the situation as amicably as possible. Unfortunately, his wife's ambivalence, which had driven Tom crazy during the marriage, was also creating havoc with the divorce process. Amy constantly changed her mind about what she wanted as a settlement. She was on her fifth lawyer, as she either fired the attorneys for not complying with her changing plan, or they dropped her as a client after she refused to sign papers that she previously had agreed to sign.

Tom said his frustration was skyrocketing, and that his children were becoming disturbed by the constant changes and controversy. Amy said she wanted the divorce and wished to get on with her life, but she continually thwarted any efforts to finalize the situation. I explained to Tom that he was in the middle of an illusion of control situation, and, therefore, rationality, logic, and effort would probably be counterproductive. Tom agreed that they hadn't worked so far. I suggested he give Amy two reasonable solutions and state that they were the only two possibilities left. Amy would have the choice as to which one was acceptable to her, but Tom should make it clear that he would not change any details of either plan. Amy could stay with her current lawyer or hire another, it didn't matter. Nothing she could do would make Tom change his offers, but the choice between them was hers. Tom said he liked the suggestion and would choose the two best agreements they had generated. He called a few weeks later to say that Amy had twisted, wriggled, and screamed, but when Tom held firm, she finally signed one of the plans.

In this case, Tom's frustration was produced by participating in an illusion of control scenario. Once Tom understood the dynamics of the situation, he was able to generate some acceptable solutions without fighting his wife for control.

SECOND-ORDER CLIENTS

Situations in which clients give a therapist total control, but are having control issues with others in their lives, can also benefit from using the transpositional model as a framework for the resolution of problems. The therapist is able to give direct information to clients about how to position themselves in relation to the control dynamics in order to reach an acceptable outcome. This technique is very useful in situations in which a compliant client appears for therapy, but the significant others in his or her life are unavailable to participate in the process. While it is always preferable to include all relevant individuals in the therapy process, it is not always possible. Distant relatives, incarcerated partners, or business associates can all have an impact on a client's life, but are not available to participate in therapy. Therapists can still achieve successful resolution of their client's problems in these situations by helping the client acquire successful ways to handle control issues in relation to these absent figures.

Reg came to my office depressed and exasperated. He had been in love with Wendy for three years. Although their relationship was healthy and intimate, the couple had never lived together because of Wendy's fear of commitment. Wendy's parents had gone through a terrible divorce when she was 12. Her mother had married and divorced twice more since that time, and her father flitted from one relationship to another. Wendy was certain that if she committed to her relationship with Reg, it would end. She loved Reg, she said, and she wanted to be with him, but she couldn't go further than that.

I asked Reg if Wendy would be willing to come into therapy with him. He sighed and said that would be very difficult, because she had just moved about 600 miles away. Reg had been pressuring Wendy to marry him, but she kept refusing. When Wendy received a job offer in another city, she decided to take it. She asked Reg to come with her, but she wouldn't consider sharing an apartment. Reg refused to move, even though he had good job prospects in that state. He couldn't see the value of following Wendy to another city if he was chasing a dead-end relationship. If Wendy were willing to commit, Reg said, he would go anywhere to be with her. Wendy called every day and had returned to see him two weekends in a row, but their visits always deteriorated into arguments about why Wendy wouldn't commit or why Reg wouldn't move. Wendy said that she wanted their relationship to continue and that she loved Reg deeply, but she was afraid of the consequences of committing.

I agreed with Reg that Wendy's underlying feelings regarding stability seemed to be interfering with her ability to commit, and I sympathized with his frustration. I suggested that perhaps he should drop any discussions of commitment or marriage, and instead concentrate on Wendy's deeper apprehensions. Reg commented that he had always been something of a free spirit, preferring free-lance work to a regular job. He prided himself on never having accumulated many material things. I asked Reg if there was any part of his life he might feel comfortable with changing, since Wendy's feelings of insecurity might be exacerbated by some aspects of his lifestyle. Reg said that he loved Wendy enough to act more responsibly, if I thought that it might make a difference. I told Reg that since I hadn't met Wendy, I couldn't be sure how she would react, but as long as Reg felt good about the changes he was making, they might be worth a try.

Reg called about a month later. He had moved to the city where Wendy lived and was working at a responsible, full-time job. Reg wasn't sure how his new, stable persona was affecting Wendy because they had stopped discussing marriage or living together, but she seemed happy to have him there. Reg did acknowledge that he was enjoying his new way of life and felt considerably less depressed and more in control.

In the preceding example, I was unable to work with both members of the relationship. The presenting client, however, gave me control within the therapeutic milieu. Because of this, I was able to make direct suggestions as to how the client could address the partial control situation in which he was involved. By having him shift to the underlying issues of his partner, instead of staying within the domain of their shared presenting problem, the client potentially could have a greater impact on the situation.

COLLEAGUES

Coworkers often solicit help, not with cases, but with their personal problems. The ethical and professional dimensions of this situation differ significantly from a supervisory relationship. Frequently, colleagues will approach a therapist because they trust their work and opinion. While they do not want to engage in a therapeutic relationship, they still seek resolution of their difficulties. In this situation, a therapist must strive to be both empathetic and detached. Because there is no therapeutic contract, and significant participants are not present, the therapist must strive to support the coworker, but not compromise the professional relationship. Once again, this sometimes can be achieved by instructing the colleague about appropriate ways in which to handle the control dynamics, rather than the specific issues, of the problem.

> Diane knocked on my door between sessions. We had
> worked together for several years in the same agency and
> frequently gave each other input about difficult cases. Diane
> was fairly distraught and asked if I had a minute to discuss
> a personal problem. Settling into a chair, she told me how
> apprehensive she was about going home for the holidays.
> Diane was part of a large family, all of whom, except her,
> lived in the same small town as her parents. Diane made it a
> point to show up for important occasions, but she always
> found the visits an ordeal because of how her parents
> treated her. While anxious for Diane to visit, they never

paid her the slightest attention once she arrived. If she tried to tell them about any event of significance in her life, her parents would ignore her and concentrate on her siblings instead. Diane found herself becoming more and more outrageous, just to provoke a reaction from her parents. When she finally achieved a suitably annoying level, her parents would tell Diane to calm down and behave herself, talking to her as if she were still a small child. Diane said she usually lost her temper at that point, leaving the room and vowing not to return. She and her parents would sometimes make up on the way to the airport at the end of the visit, but the situation always repeated itself whenever she came back. Diane was determined not to go through the scenario this year and was asking for some ideas on how to avoid it. She loved her parents, she said, and really enjoyed spending time with her siblings, but she didn't want to endure another emotional holiday.

I suggested that perhaps Diane's parents were not giving her any control in the situation, and that the more she tried to assert herself, the worse the problem became. Because they weren't open to direct approaches, Diane might try to redirect the focus to an area that everyone found acceptable—her siblings. When she went home, Diane could give all her attention to her brothers and sisters. She could stay with them or visit them extensively, direct all her news to them, and converse with them rather than with her parents. While she should treat her parents with respect, Diane should not pay them much attention, but act as if the purpose of her visit was to see her siblings. Diane said she'd give it a try, since the old interactions were certainly not working.

Diane dropped by after her visit home. She said that her parents were fairly angry when she went to stay with one of her sisters. During the holiday, however, they became solicitous of her, inquiring after her work and social life. Diane was overjoyed when her parents began talking to her, but noticed that if she were too eager to answer their queries they would start to ignore her again. She decided to concentrate on enjoying her visit with her siblings, and before long, she found she could have a decent conversation with her parents. Diane said that she didn't think the problem was solved, but that it was certainly more tolerable.

Once Diane understood that her parents were offering her no control over their relationship, she was able to position herself in a way that produced a more acceptable outcome. By redirecting the focus of the interaction away from the presenting problem and onto a mutually acceptable area of interest, Diane eventually was able to resolve some of the conflict.

OTHER PROFESSIONALS

Therapists are not the only professionals who struggle with control issues with their clientele. In any business or professional relationship, issues of cooperation and resistance affect the interaction. From medicine to sales, a practitioner is best served by adopting a position that allows a fluid, productive position with regard to other participants. Struggles for control or the adoption of an unwarranted obsequious position can lead to poor success in any interchange. By assessing the level of cooperation and control one has in a situation, one can choose the appropriate stance for a beneficial outcome.

My wife, Frances, and I would sometimes collaborate on stop-smoking cases. She would see the client for acupuncture and herbal treatment, and I would provide adjunctive hypnosis. One day, Frances called to see if I had yet seen a particular client. Sandra, a fifty-year-old woman, had already attended three acupuncture treatments. Each session began with Sandra's begging Frances to help her stop smoking. While she willingly participated with the procedures during the appointment, she always had a reason why she had been unable to stop smoking that week. Sandra's first excuse was that she had been given a huge assignment at work, which put unwieldy pressure on her. After the second appointment, Sandra said she was unable to stop because her cat needed surgery. Sandra told Frances that she could feel that the acupuncture and ear tacks were working, but that she was unable to stop because of all the tension in her life. She said she knew that there must be some other special technique that could help her. Frances was at her wit's end, vacillating between wanting to terminate the client and feeling sorry for her.

I commiserated with Frances and said that I hadn't actually met Sandra, because she had canceled all of her appointments with me because of her work overload and the cat's operation. I suggested that we had an Imperfect Client on our hands and should treat her accordingly. Frances agreed that when Sandra came in, she would tell her that she knew of no other way to help her at this time, and that Sandra would be better off spending her time paying attention to all of the things that made her want to smoke. She added that when Sandra felt she understood the problem well enough to know that it was the proper time to begin treatments, she should call us for appointments.

When Sandra heard the plan, she begged for more help now, but Frances held firm. By the time Sandra had left the office, she had agreed to concentrate on what made her want to smoke and said she would contact us when it was the right time to stop smoking. About two weeks later, we each received a call from Sandra. After keeping track of her life, she realized that there would never be a "right" time to stop smoking. Sandra was determined to quit, in spite of pressures that might dissuade her. She successfully attended a series of appointments with both of us and, as of a six-month follow-up, was still smokefree.

Professionals of many types struggle with the illusion of control clients in their practices. These clients are always better served by yielding to their control issues than by chasing their problems, a strategy that also leads to less wear and tear on the practitioner. No matter what professional specialty is involved or what type of control is being proffered, there can always be improvement in client relations if people understand the control dynamics of their clients and position themselves accordingly.

SYSTEMS

Many therapists who work in an agency setting find themselves in situations that call for an understanding of control dynamics. Interpersonal relations between administrators, staff, coworkers, and adjunctive programs create varied scenarios of authority and cooperation. The structure of transpositional therapy can be useful in helping therapists position themselves in the office milieu. Even therapists who work in a private practice setting will find the techniques helpful in interacting with partners and administrative staff. Just as family therapy was derived from a systems approach, the principles of this theory can be adapted for a system, instead of a client.

> A social worker working in a community health service came for advice. She was struggling with her team, composed primarily of medical personnel and psychologists. Gwen had been received enthusiastically by her program since she had specialized training in family therapy and a wealth of work experience. She was given a senior position and asked to help the other staff members work more effectively with families. During staff meetings, however, Gwen's suggestions were frequently ignored and often challenged, since her approach to dealing with clients was so different from that of the rest of the team. Often the other members would solicit her opinion and then discount or ridicule her ideas. If Gwen remained quiet during meetings, the team would imply

that she was being uncooperative. It seemed that they wanted Gwen's input and qualifications, but not her expertise.

I suggested that Gwen was trapped in an illusion of control situation. The team continually asked for her ideas, but refused to follow up on any of them. I framed three choices for Gwen. She could continue trying to prove to her team that her way was the right way, a choice that had not been successful previously, and was likely to be frustrating in the future. She could remove herself from the team, by not attending meetings or by meditating while they discussed problems. Finally, she could exercise her professionalism outside of the team, by liaising with other agencies who actually wanted her and valued her training. Gwen said she didn't think she could continue as she had in the past, and that she didn't want to be viewed as passive or uncooperative. She decided to make contact with other agencies in the health service who would be more willing to accept her advice. A call from Gwen several months later revealed that she still didn't receive cooperation within her own program, but that she was keeping her sanity and perspective, because of the appreciation she was receiving from personnel in other areas.

In systems, as in therapy, therapists believe they can force their way out of problems if they are simply persistent. Unfortunately, if control issues are not understood, such efforts are often unsuccessful and lead to frustration. Transpositional therapy can suggest beneficial ways for individuals to position themselves within and outside of the therapeutic context. Because the same patterns of interchange exist in any situation, understanding issues of control can lead to successful interactions in diverse circumstances. Taking an authoritative stance in a position of no control is of as little use at a sales counter as it is in a therapy room. To maximize beneficial outcomes in any interpersonal exchange, issues of authority and cooperation must be ascertained and used to make appropriate adjustments in position.

16

COMPLEX
CONTROL PATTERNS

Issues of control become considerably more complex when dealing with a family situation, as individual family members often offer a therapist different types of control. Some members are anxious to cooperate, whereas others have no interest in even attending the sessions. To add to the confusion, there are also patterns of control in the family itself. As individuals struggle to obtain, maintain, or abdicate power within the family structure, therapists find themselves having to determine their positions, not only in relation to the client, but also in regard to the shifting family dynamics. To be effective, a therapist must understand the needs of each family member relative to control issues—who has influence over whom in the family, and what has to occur for the family to have a healthier, symptom-free existence.

As if the situation itself weren't complex enough, family control patterns frequently shift across the course of therapy. A family or individual might give a therapist one type of control initially but change that position as therapy progresses. The shift might be a result of how the therapist has interacted with a certain family member, since focusing on one individual often produces changes in other family members as well. Clients who start out as cooperative might withdraw their control if they perceive that the therapist is not being sensitive to their point of view as compared with that of someone else in the family. Framing a problem in a certain way can cause increased compliance by some members, but a decrease for others. For instance, if a family comes to therapy for help with a child's temper tantrums, the parents may be cooperative until the therapist suggests that they might be responsible for instigating their child's behavior. On the other hand, their resistant child might increase his or her compliance once the child sees that he or she is not being blamed for the problem. In order to achieve a positive result, the therapists must balance their reactions to effect the desired outcome.

Therapists traditionally have attempted to achieve success in a family context by developing rapport with each family member. The therapist works toward understanding each individual's point of view in an effort to achieve cooperation from everyone involved. In many circumstances, family members welcome this forum for airing their problems, but as soon as therapy shifts into the phase where the therapist tries to challenge a position or to change dimensions within the family context, compliance disappears. Confounded, the therapist reverts to a more supportive, accepting role in an attempt to reestablish rapport. This interplay can persist for a long time, with the family never moving from its normal, homeostatic state.

Given the complexities, one might question why therapists would risk their sanity by engaging in family therapy, when they could simplify the process by concentrating on the presenting client in individual treatment. Perhaps the question can best be answered by understanding that family dynamics exist whether they are occurring in the therapy room or outside it. Freud once said that his patients would recover much faster if their families didn't bother them. The reality is that all clients must deal with family members and significant others, and the success of therapy often rests on their ability to do this in a healthy manner. It is easier for a therapist to affect positive changes in an observable system than in one where the family members are only present as "ghosts." Absent individuals give the lowest degree of control of all.

To properly assess a family's dynamics relative to control, a therapist must also determine the hierarchical structure of the family. While every member of a family can proffer a different type of control to a therapist during sessions, effective positioning cannot take place until the therapist determines how power flows within the family itself. While hierarchy is often considered a politically incorrect topic for discussion, it cannot be denied that in any interaction, someone has more influence and someone else has less. No matter how we strive for respect and equality in our relationships, at any given time, on any given issue, someone has more control. To position themselves effectively within a family context, therapists must know who holds power over whom. Without knowing whether a child, a parent, or a grandparent exerts the most influence at a certain time or in a particular situation, the therapist becomes helpless to know at what level to intervene.

Therapists must determine not only the form of the hierarchy, but the cause of control patterns as well. Do children have power over their parents because they receive no discipline or because they have a disability that makes the parents reluctant to intervene? Is a spouse powerless over his or her partner because that spouse has less status or because depression renders him or her immobile? When therapists understand both the structure of a family and the cause of its dynamics, they have a better chance of intervening in an effective manner.

The quality of power within the family is also significant. A family member might hold control in one situation, but not in another. Sometimes individuals share authority, whereas in other cases the power is absolute. Some hierarchical structures seem inviolate, while others are more contextual or casual. The therapist must determine the strength and flexibility of power within the family, and in the family's attitude toward the therapist, before a suitable plan of action can be formulated.

The previous chapters focused on how a therapist can respond to an individual or family that offers a single type of control during therapy. Using the guides of transpositional therapy, a therapist can select appropriate stances, hooks, and tools to help clients meet their goals. While the principles remain the same in a multidimensional control situation, the therapist needs simultaneously to consider a number of other factors.

METHOD

In a complex control system, where members of a family present with multifaceted control issues regarding the therapist and themselves, the following strategy is useful.

1. Ascertain the type of control each individual in the family is presenting to the therapist.

   Using the guidelines of previous chapters, the therapist can assess the type of cooperation each of the family members is bringing to the therapy context. By evaluating their behavior during pretherapy conversations, information from referral sources, and their actions during the first session, a therapist can determine the type of control (total control, partial control, no control, or illusion of control) each participant is offering.

2. Estimate the quality of the control offered.

    The therapist should ascertain not only the pattern of control he or she is being given, but also the strength of that control. Some participants will offer the therapist total control, without a strong commitment. Others seem resistant at first, but are easily pacified. The therapist should try to determine how firmly the individual is invested in his or her stance. This can often be observed by assessing how each participant reacts to a direct suggestion.

3. Determine the hierarchical relationship of the participants.

    Before a successful strategy can be devised, the therapist needs to understand the power structure of the participants. The matter of who seems to have the most control within the system should be assessed, and any coalitions of power should be investigated. Hierarchical positions can be either overt or covert. In either case, it is possible to achieve resolution within a family by successfully changing one key member. This is not always the person with the most power, but the one who is in the best position to effect a change. If intervention is directed to a pivotal point in the hierarchy, improvement can have wide-ranging consequences, as family members alter their relationships to each other and to the therapist.

4. Determine the cause of the hierarchical relationships.

    As mentioned earlier, the cause of the dynamics within a family can be as important as the structure itself. An individual might have more status in the family because that person makes more money, is more intelligent, has better interpersonal skills, or simply is free of symptoms. Persons who hold power within a system either may be responsible for generating the pathology or are a potential mechanism for fixing it. The better the therapist understands the family dynamics, the more accurate a solution can be found, especially since these issues are often related to the presenting and underlying problems.

5. Analyze the pattern of control in the context of the family hierarchy in order to formulate a plan for therapy.

Once the initial patterns of control and power dynamics have been determined, the therapist can formulate the most appropriate strategy for intervention. An individual or set of participants can be identified as primary targets, and the therapist can select the appropriate hooks, levers, and tools to invest them in the process and resolve their problems. Because the interplay between therapist and family, control issues and hierarchy, is so complex, there is often no single answer to a family's problem. The therapist stands within a multidimensional weave, where pulling any thread creates a significant change in the fabric. Although there are many possible ways to handle each case, some are more likely to be successful than others. It is often the artistry of the therapist, and the ability and willingness to change course when necessary, that will optimize success and minimize frustration.

CASE EXAMPLES

The following section illustrates how complex cases can be handled within the model. Individuals will be designated in terms of the control they offer the therapist. For ease of illustration, total control will be abbreviated as TC, partial control as PC, no control as NC, and illusion of control as IC. The person who has the most power in the family hierarchy will be at the top of the client pyramid.

Family A

Brenda came to therapy with her husband, Chuck, and 14-year-old daughter, Cindy. She was concerned that Cindy was seeing an older boy and was sexually involved with him. Brenda complained that since Cindy had started seeing this boy, her grades had gone down and she'd abandoned her close friends. Cindy made it clear during the session that she had no intention to end the relationship with this boy, and that nothing that occurred in therapy was going to change her mind. Chuck wanted to see his daughter's relationship with the boy terminated, but he was worried that Cindy would run away from home if they put too much pressure on her. Brenda felt that none of this would be happening if Chuck drank less and was a more responsible father. She said that she was tired of taking responsibility for everything in the family and wanted me to fix things so that she wasn't always in charge. Chuck said that he didn't know what his drinking had to do with Cindy's sexual behavior, but he desperately wanted some relief from all the bickering that was taking place at home.

From the initial interview, it appeared the family had the following dynamics.

Brenda, the mother (TC)

Chuck, the father (PC)   Cindy, the daughter (NC)

The presenting problem was Cindy's behavior, with underlying issues involving her father's drinking and the parent's hierarchical relationship. To be effective, the therapy needed to use the control the parents were offering in way that would invest Cindy in the process. Even though an authoritarian approach was possible, given Brenda and Chuck's cooperation, it clearly could not be directed toward Cindy, who was offering no control. There was more chance of success if the intervention redirected Cindy to an issue where she was willing to yield more control.

I asked Cindy if her father's drinking was important to her. She said she loved her father very much but hated how much he drank. She found it impossible to talk to Chuck because of how withdrawn he became after a six pack of beer. Cindy used to bring her homework to her father to check, but that had become increasingly futile, since he was often too hazy to be of any help.

I asked Chuck if he would be willing to make a deal with Cindy. He would restrict his drinking to those nights when Cindy was out with her boyfriend. In that way, he wouldn't be interfering with Cindy's school work or her desire to talk with him. Any night that Cindy stayed home, Chuck would abstain. Cindy could help her father by spending more time concentrating on her homework or inviting her friends over for the evening, since Chuck would spend less time drinking. The family agreed to the plan.

In this case, by attending to the family's control issues, as well as their presenting and underlying problems, an intervention was designed that also dealt with the family's hierarchical structure. There was no struggle for control with Cindy, since the focus was moved off of her and onto an issue with which she was willing to cooperate. Chuck was invested into the process by addressing the underlying issues regarding his drinking in a way that would help his daughter, and Brenda's position in the family hierarchy was balanced by making Chuck more responsible for the family's well-being.

Family B

Tom, age 16, and his parents, Frank and Gina, attended the first session together. The parents had recently separated after years of arguing. However, their dissension had not stopped with the marriage. Tom became so frustrated with his parents' constant bickering that he once put his fist through a wall to get them to stop. Tom said that he was really sorry about his behavior, and didn't mean to act badly, but it was the only way he knew to get his parents to stop fighting. Gina expressed concern over Tom's aggression, but said she was unable to keep her feelings under control. She indicated that she still was angry about how Frank had treated her during their marriage, and that she had no intention of having him push her around now that she'd managed to escape.

Gina was willing to entertain ways of helping Tom, as long as they didn't involve her kowtowing to his father. Frank said that Gina and Tom's behavior was a perfect example of how messed up they really were. He begged me to help his son before the boy did some real damage. Whenever I suggested a way that Frank might help Tom, however, he complained about how overloaded he was with work and that he didn't really have any time to carry out a plan. Frank wanted me to fix the problem, though. He said that he cared about his son, but was too busy to work on the problem himself.

In this case, the following pattern appeared prevalent.

Tom, the son (TC)

Gina, the mother (PC)   Frank, the father (IC)

It is not unusual for an adolescent to be in a hierarchically superior position to the parents, especially when the child's symptomatology is severe and the parents' relationship is fragmented. In this situation, Tom wanted help with his problems, but he could not understand how to stop his parents from arguing without acting aggressively. His only power came from his parents' fear. Tom's mother was willing to cooperate in therapy because she cared about her son, but her participation was conditioned on the fact that I wouldn't ask her to act conciliatory toward her ex-husband. Frank's control was illusory in that he wanted his son's problems to be resolved, but his cooperation disappeared whenever he was asked to act on his son's behalf.

I decided to use Tom's total control in a way that addressed his mother's underlying issues regarding the separation, as well as his father's control issues. I suggested that Frank be the sole target of Tom's anger. Whenever his son felt overwhelmed by his frustration, he was to yell at Frank on the phone. If Frank was too busy to talk or was away from home on business, Tom was to shout an appropriate message into the answering machine.

This intervention strove to use the family's control dynamics in a way that addressed both their presenting and underlying problems. Tom was given a direct instruction because he willingly gave control of his problem to the therapist. He was told to direct his anger toward his parents in a way that was acceptable to all of them. Gina was able to align herself with her son's anger toward his father, without needing to control him, which increased her status. Frank felt as though he was contributing to his son's well-being, although he was actually doing nothing active to help him, and he thereby gained a boost in position as well. The family's presenting and underlying issues and their hierarchical pattern were all addressed by adopting an appropriate position in relation to their dynamics.

Family C

Don and his wife, Shirley, brought their child, Matt, age eight, to therapy to solve his lying problems. Matt had begun lying about a year ago, but the situation was growing steadily worse. He recently stole some money from Shirley, something he'd never done before. Matt started crying during his mother's report and said that he didn't want to act this way, but that he just couldn't stop. Shirley began weeping as well, stating that the whole family was falling apart, that nothing was the same since she found out two months previously that Don was involved in a relationship with another woman. Don snorted, and said that his affair had nothing to do with it, that he was here to help Matt, not to deal with his own infidelities. Don said he couldn't understand what all the fuss was about, anyway, since all children lie. He added that he had lied when he was a boy, and was sure that I had as well. Don thought all the concern over Matt was silly, and he'd only come along because his wife had told him to.

It appeared that the following dynamics were present in the family.

Shirley, the mother (PC)

Don, the father (NC)   Matt, the child (TC)

Shirley held the dominant position, since she clearly had enough authority to make both Don and Matt appear for therapy. She also controlled her husband and son by instilling guilt about their misbe-havior. While Shirley wanted to help her son, her involvement in the therapy situation was attenuated by her marital problems. Don was clearly uninterested in participating in therapy, as he didn't think either he or his son had a problem, and Matt wanted help but had no power on his own to get better. It didn't seem prudent to elucidate for Don that Matt's stealing was a metaphor for his own dishonest behavior. Likewise, I did not feel that addressing Matt's stealing would resolve what was essentially a marital issue.

I asked Don what changes he would like to see in his wife and son. Don said that he felt that his wife didn't value him as a person and didn't spend any time with him. He said that Shirley never let him dis-cipline his son, and that she didn't seem to appreciate him as a husband. I asked Shirley if she would consider letting Don be more involved with his son, and that perhaps the two of them could plan some activi-ties where they could be more like a couple and a family. Don said he had some leave coming from work, and he'd love for the three of them to get away and just have some fun for a change. Shirley said she would consider the idea if Don gave up his relationship with the other woman, and he agreed to end his affair if Shirley would spend more time with him. Once the couple agreed to terms, Matt was given the responsibility of reporting on how the family was doing when they returned each session. His parents would truthfully report their progress to Matt, and he would responsibly relay it to the therapist.

In this situation, the intervention was directed to the underlying issues in a way that would invest both Shirley, who was giving partial control, and Don, who was giving no control. By addressing the mari-tal problems in a way that did not increase resistance in Don, the cou-ple was able to work toward resolving their problems. The presenting problem, Matt's lying, was made an implicit goal, with his parents used as models for improving his behavior.

Family D

A 15-year-old girl, Maria, was referred for therapy by a child protection agency. Maria had run away from a shelter for the third time that month. A session involving Maria, her grandmother, her mother, her twin sister, and an ex-stepfather was set up. Maria's grandmother, Inez, took charge of the proceedings from the beginning. Inez said she felt that Maria's mother had been unfairly treated by the child protection agency and believed Maria's only reason for running away from the shelter was that she wanted to go home. Inez made it clear that she felt my sole function was to facilitate a reconciliation in the family by proving to the agency that her daughter was capable of caring for the girl.

Maria remained quiet during her grandmother's instructions. When I asked Maria what she herself wanted to accomplish during the session, she said that she loved her mother and sister very much and missed them when she was away. Her placement in the shelter resulted from several incidents of abuse by her mother's current husband.* Maria said that she was sorry for the trouble she had caused in the family and tried to apologize to her mother by bringing her flowers every time she ran away from the shelter.

Whenever I tried to speak to Lorena, Maria's mother, the grandmother would intervene. Inez said that there was no need to bring up anything from the past, because my job was to make everything right for her daughter and grandchildren's future. Inez said that Lorena cherished her daughters and couldn't bear to be away from them. During the session, however, it became evident that, while Lorena loved the twins, she felt they were putting a strain on her marriage. She evidently felt that it would be much easier if her daughters weren't at home so she could devote her time to her current husband and their children.

Marlena, Maria's twin sister, also was highly ambivalent. She spoke of missing her sister, but made it clear that life in the home was more pleasant without Maria. This was due to the fact that Lorena often played the girls off each other, accepting Maria and rejecting Marlena, or doting on Marlena and ignoring Maria. When Maria was away, Marlena received much more attention. Marlena held her sister's hand during the session, but she would bristle if anyone else focused on Maria.

Julian, Lorena's last husband, had lived with the family for eight years. Although he wasn't the girls' biological father, he cared deeply for the twins, and was anxious to help in any way possible. Julian lived in another state, but he returned for the meeting, because he cared so much for Maria.

---

*He was not attending the sessions at the request of the care and protection agency.

From the first session, the dynamics of the family appeared to be as follows:

Inez, the grandmother (PC)

Maria (TC)	Marlena (IC)	Lorena (IC)	Julian (TC)
	the twin	the mother	the stepfather

Inez was clearly in charge of the family, but she was only willing to participate in therapy if I supported her idea of how it should take place. Maria was highly conciliatory toward me and everyone else in the family. Both Lorena and Marlena seemed interested in cooperating with me to help Maria, but their control became illusory in light of the ambivalence caused by their own agendas. Julian was willing to do whatever was necessary to help me or Maria.

I decided to invest the grandmother into therapy by emphasizing her underlying wish for everyone in her family to be happy. We discussed how Lorena's struggle with the girls was straining her current marriage and her ability to cope. To give Lorena a chance to make this present relationship work, Maria could live with Julian and his new family, and Marlena could move in with her grandmother. Inez would be the focal point of the family (a position she already held) and ensure that everyone maintained communication with each other. The plan was readily accepted by all participants. Lorena could concentrate on her new husband and children, Julian was pleased to be able to help Maria, Maria was happy to live with Julian and ease the strain on her mother's marriage, Marlena was content not to struggle for her mother's attention and knew she could depend on her grandmother's affection, and Inez was able to keep her family together, even if at a distance, while supporting her daughter. The intervention allowed all of the individuals to meet their goals without compromising Maria's safety or creating resistance.

Family E

Philip, a seven-year-old boy diagnosed with the Attention-Deficit/ Hyperactivity Syndrome (AD/HD), appeared for therapy with his mother, Vivian, and his grandmother, Charlotte. Dr. Jones, the developmental pediatrician managing the case, was worried about Philip's behavior following the recent birth of his baby brother. Philip engaged in wild actions around the infant and had tried to harm his brother on several occasions. Dr. Jones felt that Philip's hyperactive behavior was adequately managed by medication, but was concerned about the strong emotional reaction caused by the arrival of a new sibling.

Vivian said that she could not understand why they were referred for family therapy since Philip's uncontrolled behavior was clearly a product of his AD/HD. There was no point in her trying to correct or manage Philip, she pointed out, since his syndrome prohibited him from being able to control himself. Even Philip agreed that, because he had AD/HD, he couldn't be held responsible for his actions toward the baby. Charlotte, the grandmother, said she wasn't so sure. She was from the old school and believed there was little that couldn't be fixed by a firm hand.

I offered several suggestions, including the idea that someone needed to watch Philip at all times around the baby. Vivian rejected all of my ideas and added that she was too exhausted from her recent delivery and having to deal with a hyperactive child to monitor Philip's behavior. Her husband worked long hours and couldn't supervise the boy. Charlotte offered her help, but Vivian said that Philip's grandmother didn't have the expertise to work with an AD/HD child properly.

From the first session, the family constellation appeared to be the following.

Vivian, the mother (NC)

Philip, the son (NC)   Charlotte, the grandmother (PC)

Vivian and Philip were clearly too tied to his diagnosis to yield control during therapy. Charlotte was anxious to help, but was restricted by her own views toward Philip's syndrome and her unilateral way of thinking about discipline. Because the mother's stance of no control led her to reject any direct suggestions, I decided that the best approach would be to exaggerate the underlying problem, Philip's AD/HD. I commiserated with Vivian's dismissal of her mother's help, stating that in a case of a child with attentional problems as severe as Philip's, no one stood a chance of correcting his behavior. I offered several other suggestions, and then discounted each of them as being inadequate for a boy as involved as Philip. Vivian stated that she was capable of handling Philip's behavior, if he were away from the baby. Charlotte said she had never appreciated the seriousness of Philip's condition, and that while she might not be able to handle her grandson, perhaps she could watch the baby while Vivian took Philip somewhere else. I expressed concern as to whether Vivian, in her currently fatigued state, would be overpowered by her hyperactive son, but she assured me that she was more than capable of handling Philip.

When the family returned for the next session, there was a marked improvement. Philip said his mother had taken him to his favorite restaurant and a movie during the week. He admitted that he really enjoyed himself and decided that sharing life with a new sibling wouldn't be so bad. Vivian was also more enthusiastic. After spending time with Philip during the week, Vivian felt that his AD/HD wasn't as severe as it used to be. She said she was amazed that when Philip became rowdy during the movie and she asked him to calm down, he actually became quiet. Charlotte said she had enjoyed the time with her new grandchild, but that she was exhausted when she got home, and it made her appreciate what Vivian went through in a day.

In this situation, Vivian and Philip initially gave me no control because his syndrome, AD/HD, held all the power. By yielding to their views and then exaggerating the condition, Vivian and Philip were able to resist the diagnosis instead of the therapist. The magnification of Philip's syndrome also allowed Charlotte to be more supportive of her daughter.

Family F

Otto appeared for therapy with his wife, Nicola, and his stepdaughter, Amanda, 15 years of age. Amanda had accused Otto of sexually molesting her, and the family was in turmoil. Nicola insisted that Otto move out until the issue was addressed. Amanda was furious at her mother for insisting that the family all come to therapy together. Five minutes into the session, she bolted out of the room, with Nicola in pursuit.

Otto watched them go and then sank into his chair. When I asked him what had happened sexually between him and Amanda, he insisted that he couldn't remember anything of that kind. Otto joked that perhaps he had a split personality, one half that did that sort of thing without the other half's knowing. He said that the only reason he was attending the session was because he was afraid that his wife and stepdaughter would press charges. After several more attempts to get information were met with evasion, I asked Otto to sit in the waiting room while I spoke to Nicola and Amanda.

Amanda dissolved in tears as soon as we began to talk. She recounted her story and begged me to help her get over this terrible event. I asked her if she would be willing to tell her story to Otto, to help him remember what happened. Amanda said she wanted nothing to do with her stepfather and would not sit in the room with him. Nicola looked very uncomfortable while Amanda was talking. She said she was torn between caring for her daughter and helping her husband with his problem. Nicola said that she believed that Amanda's safety was paramount, but that she wanted the family to have therapy to see if resolution was possible. Nicola also couldn't understand why Amanda was so adamant about not participating with Otto during the session when she was comfortable inviting him to the house for supper or to watch a video. Amanda said that she asked Otto to come over because she really still liked him, but that the idea of discussing these issues with him was intolerable.

It appeared that the family constellation presented during therapy was as follows:

Amanda, the daughter (IC)

Otto, the stepfather (NC)   Nicola, the mother (PC)

Amanda was clearly in charge of the family due to the severity of her symptoms. She presented an illusion of control in that she refused to comply with the structure of therapy but maintained a relationship with her stepfather outside of the sessions. Otto was not interested in cooperating at all, and was actually an involuntary client. Nicola wanted to help her daughter, but felt obligated to her husband.

I suggested to Amanda that she had only three choices in this situation. She could invite Otto into the therapy with her and try to work on their issues; she could continue as before, seeing Otto outside the therapy room but not working toward resolving their problem, or she could avoid seeing Otto altogether. Amanda started crying and said that she had only invited Otto over the house to please her mother, and and that she really wanted him out of their lives. Nicola put her arm around her daughter. She said that her own family, which lived in another state, had invited her and Amanda to stay with them, and that she could better handle the dissolution of her marriage with the support of people who loved her. She asked Amanda if moving to her grandparents' house was acceptable. Amanda said she would probably miss her friends if they moved, but she actually felt better knowing that Otto was in another state.

Otto was furious when he learned of his family's decision. He insisted that he had no memory of anything Amanda had reported. I asked him if he would like to work toward remembering the events. Otto said that if he found out that he actually had molested the girl, he would kill himself, so he might just as well not know. I suggested that if Otto were feeling suicidal, we could work on some other problem instead. He said that he wanted help in dealing with his loneliness and feelings of isolation. After a month of therapy working on these issues, Otto mentioned that he would probably feel less alone if he reestablished a connection with his first wife and his children. He said that he didn't want to risk acting badly with his biological daughter, however, and he asked me if I would help him learn to establish proper boundaries for his behavior with her.

In this case, Amanda's illusion of control took precedence because of her emotional distress and need for protection. Concrete alternatives helped her to establish a choice without struggling with her control issues. Nicola's own ambivalence disappeared in light of Amanda's decision, and she was empowered to find a solution that worked for both her and her daughter. Otto's stance of no control was handled by redirecting therapy to a topic that would invest him in the process without causing further resistance. Since Amanda was safe in another state with her mother, there was not as much urgency to address Otto's presenting problem. Once a sufficient level of trust was generated by helping Otto with his other issues, he was able to give me the control to deal with his problem of appropriate behavior with young girls.

Family therapy situations often present as multifaceted control problems. In addition to offering multiple types of control to a therapist, a family also has a number of interpersonal dynamics that can affect the course of therapy. By addressing the hierarchy and degree of power within the family, in the context of control patterns presented during therapy, therapists can position themselves to achieve a greater probability of success.

17

SUMMARY
AND CONCLUSIONS

In the preceding chapters, ideas were presented for how therapists can effectively position themselves during therapy in relation to the control issues their clients present. The transpositional approach to therapy synthesizes the rationale behind both therapist-directed and client-driven models of therapy. In this system, the therapists have the expertise and judgment that allow therapy to be both productive and effective. Their position, however, depends on the characteristics of their clients. Therapists in the transpositional model can be both expert and supporter. They are willing to direct therapy, but in a manner that is both respectful of and responsive to the individual needs of their clients.

Some systems of therapy demand cooperation and screen prospective clients to see whether they are "ready," "invested," or "motivated." Others capitalize on resistance and pattern their interventions to maximize a struggle. Clients who do not fit the therapist's expectations are forced into a mold or discharged from treatment. Given that outcome studies find that all systems generally produce a 60 percent success rate, there is a need to go beyond the boundaries of therapy style so that a greater number of clients can be helped.

Outcome studies also indicate that the qualities of a particular therapist affect that therapist's level of success. Obviously, therapists who are warm and engaging will produce a more positive response from clients than will ones who are nasty and condescending. The transpositional approach takes these dynamics one step further, however. Some clients give a therapist total control if they perceive them as being supportive, but others may need a therapist to act authoritatively before they can cooperate. In order for a therapist to achieve success with an individual client, the therapist must be sensitive to the information revealed by that client over the course of treatment, instead of adopting a singular stance prescribed by a particular theory.

Often, therapists who operate from a specific theoretical orientation behave in a prescribed manner because they know it to be "right." Clients who do not fit into their model are labeled as difficult or incurable. Instead of evaluating their performance on the basis of whether the client is being helped, they hold to their theoretical dogma, because they are certain it is the best and most effective way of interacting with clients. The situation is analogous to that of clients who enter therapy enmeshed in a relationship or course of action driven by a particular philosophy. Even when such clients see their behavior as unsatisfying or destructive, they are unable to deviate from their actions because they are dedicated to their belief system. They will admit their misery, but insist it is produced by the fact that the rest of the world does not understand what is right. In much the same way, therapists who commit to a single course of action with a client, because they know it is the optimal way to respond, remain dedicated to their approach even if it meets with dismal success. They blame their failure on the client, society, or karma, without realizing that the "best" in best practice is a relative, and not an absolute, concept.

By what justification are we, as therapists, allowed to decide the approach that a client needs? Surely, clients have the right to their own positions and issues. It is the therapist's responsibility to respect the differences of individual clients and adjust himself or herself accordingly. Adopting a unilateral approach to clients, because it is considered the proper course of action, rejects the concept that clients are unique individuals requiring different modes of treatment. It is not surprising that many systems of therapy achieve limited success if clients are expected to conform to their notion of best practice.

The transpositional model encourages therapists to be flexible in their positions relative to their clients' control issues. This adaptation of response reduces frustration in the therapist while increasing success for the client. These alterations, however, should be distinguished from being overly solicitous or pandering. It is not an attempt to please clients at all costs, or even make them happy. In fact, the therapist's stance at times might not seem supportive to the client, especially if the therapist is taking an authoritative or exaggerated position. Fluctuations of stance are geared toward achieving clients' goals, not necessarily making them feel warm and fuzzy.

I once worked with a child psychotherapist who could not care enough for her clients. All of her actions were driven by the desire to increase her clients' happiness quotient. She took them to fast-food restaurants, showered them with candy, instructed their parents on how to make the children feel better, and pounced on anyone causing the slightest emotional distress in a child. The psychotherapist was continually rewarded with drawings, presents, and hugs from the children. Undeniably, the children were happy. Unfortunately, in many cases, they also often didn't get better. The children continued as victims, despite feeling happier, and never made the transition to more successful functioning.

This is not to say that a therapist should ignore a client's feelings. It is only that sometimes a hard, direct line produces a better result for the client. Therapists who continually take a one-down position in relation to their clients may make their clients comfortable, but they often lose the ability to effect change. Since the clients do not respect the therapist's ability to have a point of view, they see the therapist as an extension of their own faulty system. Therapists must know when to take control and when to lose it.

Therapists are as unique as are their clients. They bring a wide range of strengths and weaknesses to each session. Since transpositional therapy requires a therapist to be a chameleon, it is useful to identify areas where a particular therapist might have difficulty and where that therapist has specific strengths. Some therapists are very good at taking control, whereas others have a talent for yielding. To adjust successfully to a client's control pattern, a therapist must be competent at both.

The following checklist is meant to be a guide for therapists, to identify the style they use most often and to target those areas in which they might seek to improve. As you go through the list, check the items that are typically part of your therapeutic practice.

_____ Gives clear suggestions to clients during therapy

_____ Makes direct statements to clients

_____ Believes that the therapist understands problems more clearly than do the clients

_____ Asks content-directed questions of clients

_____ Asks insight-directed questions of clients

_____ Prefers to ask for the client's view rather than to express own opinion

_____ Prefers the client to direct the course of treatment

_____ Typically deals with clients from the perspective of a single theoretical model

_____ Develops a working hypothesis and pursues it through the course of treatment

_____ Changes direction when the therapy is not succeeding

_____ Dismisses resistive clients

_____ Ignores resistance in clients

_____ Encourage resistance in clients

_____ Requires cooperation from clients for the method to be successful

The items in the list are not intended to be diagnostic or exhaustive, but should give therapists an idea of which components of practice they find most desirable and which they might have difficulty in achieving.

As therapists, our primary responsibility is the successful resolution of our clients' problems. The transpositional approach seeks to maximize positive outcomes, while making the therapeutic experience more pleasant, and less frustrating, for all involved. The technique is not infallible. Such issues as therapist competence, external circumstances, and a client's secondary gains from a problem will always need to be factored into success. A transpositional approach to therapy simply maximizes a therapist's own capacities and provides insight into possibly useful strategies.

One therapist, when hearing of this model, asserted he never encountered control difficulties in his clients. I wish I had his practice. In all seriousness, one could probably eliminate all control problems by always being conciliatory. However, that approach does not always lead to success in therapy or meet the needs of clients who desire direction. As therapists, we need to accept and respect our clients' differences and responsibly, professionally, work to achieve their goals.

REFERENCES

Allgood, S.M., Bischoff, R.I., Smith, T.A., & Salts, C.J. (1992). Therapist interventions: do they really influence client resistance? *The American Journal of Family Therapy, 20*, 333–340.

Beutler, L.E., & Consoli, A.J. (1993). Matching the therapist's interpersonal stance to clients' characteristics: Contributions from systematic eclectic psychotherapy. *Psychotherapy, 30*, 417–422.

Beutler, L.E., Engle, D., Mohr, D., Daldrup, R.J., Bergan, J., Meredith, K., & Merry, W. (1991). Predictors of differential and self directed psychotherapeutic procedures. *Journal of Consulting and Clinical Psychology, 59*, 333–340.

Carr, A. (1990). Failure in family therapy: A catalogue of engagement mistakes. *Journal of Family Therapy, 12*, 371–386.

De Shazer, S. (1988). *Investigating solutions in brief therapy*. New York: Norton.

Erickson, M. (1964). The burden of responsibility in effective psychotherapy. *American Journal of Clinical Hypnosis, 6*, 269–271.

Erickson, M. (1976). Techniques for resistant patients. In J. Haley (Ed.), *Advanced techniques of hypnosis and therapy* (p. 472). New York: Grune & Stratton.

Fisch, R., Weakland, J.H., & Segal, L. (1982). *The tactics of change: Doing therapy briefly*. San Francisco: Jossey-Bass.

Gilligan, S. (1987). *Therapeutic trances*. New York: Brunner/Mazel.

Goldner, V. (1993). Power and hierarchy: Let's talk about it! *Family Process, 32*, 157–162.

Haley, J. (1963). *Strategies of psychotherapy*. New York: Grune & Stratton.

Haley, J. (1976). *Advanced techniques of hypnosis and therapy*. New York: Grune & Stratton.

Haley, J. (1987). *Problem solving therapy*. San Francisco: Jossey-Bass.

Kolden, G.G., Howard, K.I., & Maling, M.S. (1994). The counseling relationship and treatment process and outcome. *The Counseling Psychologist, 22*, 82–89.

Langer, E.J. *The Psychology of Control*. (1983). New York: Sage Publications.

Lao Tsu (1971). *Tao te ching*. New York: Vintage Books.

Madanes, C. (1981). *Strategic family therapy*. San Francisco: Jossey-Bass.

Miller, S., Hubble, M., & Duncan, B. (1995). No more bells and whistles. *Family Therapy Networker*, March/April, 53–63.

Minuchin, S. (1991). The seductions of constructivism. *Family Therapy Networker*, September/October, 47–50.

Seligman, M.E.P. *Helplessness: On depression, development and death*. San Francisco: Freeman (1975)

Whiston, S.C., & Sexton, T.L. (1993). An overview of psychotherapy outcome research: Implications for practice. *Professional Psychology: Research and Practice, 24*, 43–51.

Windle, R., & Samko, M. (1992). Hypnosis, Ericksonian hypnosis, and aikido. *American Journal of Clinical Hypnosis, 34*, 261–270.

INDEX